The Joshua Generation

Winning Your Children for Kingdom Purposes

Sue Curran

 Unless otherwise identified, Scripture quotations are from the King James Version of the Bible.

Other Scripture quotations are from the New International Version (NIV), the American Standard Version (ASV), and the New American Standard (NAS).

Take note that the name satan and related names are not capitalized. We choose not to acknowledge him, even to the point of violating grammatical rules.

Treasure House
An Imprint of
Destiny Image
P.O. Box 310
Shippensburg, PA 17257

"For where your treasure is
there will your heart be also." Matthew 6:21

ISBN 1-56043-827-4

For Worldwide Distribution
Printed in the U.S.A.

Treasure House books are available through these fine distributors outside the United States:

Christian Growth, Inc.
Jalan Kilang-Timor, Singapore 0315

Lifestream
Nottingham, England

Rhema Ministries Trading
Randburg, South Africa

Salvation Book Centre
Petaling, Jaya, Malaysia

Successful Christian Living
Capetown, Rep. of South Africa

Vision Resources
Ponsonby, Auckland, New Zealand

WA Buchanan Company
Geebung, Queensland, Australia

Word Alive
Niverville, Manitoba, Canada

Inside the U.S., call toll free to order:
1-800-722-6774

The Joshua Generation

Winning Your Children
for Kingdom Purposes

Dedicated to:

My Mother

who understood what it meant to love and nurture her children, and, together with my delightful father, give them a childhood worth remembering.

Contents

Chapter		Page
	Foreword	ix
	Introduction	xi
1	**We Have a Destiny**	1
2	**The Joshua Generation**	13
3	**It's Never Too Soon**	29
4	**Winning Their Hearts**	41
5	**Doing What Comes Naturally**	51
6	**The Loss of Childhood**	63
7	**As a Man Thinketh**	77
8	**Peace in My Day**	89
9	**The Kingdom Is Exciting!**	101
10	**What If It Doesn't Work?**	111
11	**A Handful of Keys**	123

Foreword

When Moses bargained with Pharaoh for the release of God's chosen people, Egypt's king finally agreed to release only the *men* to go into the wilderness to worship Jehovah. Moses completely rejected this offer saying, "There shall not an hoof be left behind." (See Exodus 10:26.) Moses demanded that Pharaoh release the men, women, children, and cattle to the service of the Lord.

Far too often, even in the midst of revival, churches, and even parents, are willing to leave the children behind. Perhaps there is a subconscious feeling that the children will not understand the things of God, or perhaps the adults don't want to be bothered with bringing the little ones into prayer, praise, worship, and holy living. Whatever the reason, it is far too common to see the second generation lacking knowledge in the things of God. They know how to play religion, but they don't know how to serve the Lord with gladness, simply because no one has ever taught them how.

I would like to believe that the reason both the parents and the Church abandon the children to fleshly activities is a lack of knowledge in how to bring the children into a personal experience with Christ Jesus. This book will help teach parents how to do this with as much ease as teaching a child to tie his or her shoes.

Sue Curran has a uniqueness in her church. The children are treated as persons and are participants in the prayer meetings, worship services, and church activities. I have repeatedly been thrilled to have the children of the congregation volunteer to pray for me before I preached. Their faith is pure, their fervor is refreshing, and they are completely comfortable in praying for and with an adult. This came about by design, not by accident.

An examination of our attitudes toward the spiritual lives of our children is overdue. *The Joshua Generation* will be a spotlight, both on our hearts and on the pathway before us. Its principles have worked for one congregation. Why not give them a try?

Judson Cornwall, Th.D.

Introduction

The world is in transition. Everything is in motion. Change is everywhere. It is said that nothing is as constant as change. This fact is more evident now than at any time in recent history. The global climatic conditions are in turmoil, the economic balance is in conversion, the political equation in all nations is under reformation, ideologies are deteriorating, and the future seems to be uncertain. Change is a natural characteristic of living things, for living things grow, and growth demands transition. However, the dynamics and impact of change can be either positive or negative.

From a biblical perspective, the unfolding of God's eternal purpose for man and His creation throughout history is marked by the progressive nature of change, growth, transition, and metamorphosis.

The dynamic nature of God's plan for restoration and reconciliation of His fallen man follows the pattern that He demonstrated in His dealings with the children of Israel and their progress from slavery, to deliverance, to freedom. The critical point of transition for this nation, which is a prototype of every nation, was the transfer of authority, leadership, and responsibility from Moses to Joshua, from the old to the young, from one generation to the next.

I am convinced that we are in this critical season of transition in our generation. It is the season of moving from being a child to becoming an adult, from fear to faith, from irresponsibility to responsibility, from immaturity to maturity, and from follower to leader. In essence we are moving from the wilderness to Canaan, from deliverance to freedom.

In *The Joshua Generation,* Sue Curran graphically presents this subject with skill and simple depth. She brings the reader to the critical point of understanding our responsibility for an effective transition, especially as it relates to the preparation of the next generation for their role and purpose. *The Joshua Generation* brings into focus the crucial issue of destiny and the need to capture a sense of purpose for the next generation.

Pastor Curran makes us aware of the fact that hidden in every nation is a generation, even as the generation of Joshua was hidden in the nation of Moses. In her thoughtful and thought-provoking manner, she illuminates the subject and draws us into the action of taking responsibility for the next generation. It is my earnest prayer that you will be stirred to aggressively accept the mandate to pursue the maturity of character that the next phase of ministry, during this transition, is requiring of us.

May you also commit to prepare others to take their place in the mature twenty-first century Church. Let us arise and cross the river that separates us from our land of promise and responsibility, releasing once again, in our day, the spirit of *The Joshua Generation.*

Dr. Myles Munroe
Nassau, Bahamas

Chapter 1

We Have a Destiny

Michael was only four years old when he asked the pastor if he could please speak a word to the congregation. He came to the platform during the Sunday evening worship service preceding a large conference that was to begin that week. The visiting speaker groaned in disbelief as the pastor quieted the musicians so that Michael's high-pitched little voice could be heard. The congregation listened expectantly as the child clutched the microphone and drew a deep breath.

"The Lord that reigns the earth is in our midst," Michael began. He paused as if to hear the next sentence, then continued, "...and all things shall be all right in the Lord. We shall rejoice for all the weeks that we have waited for this conference." The words began to come more forcefully now. "It shall be known that the Lord has been in our hearts and we will sing our shouts to the Lord!" Then with decided finality he declared, "With the Lord's help we can defeat our enemy. With God as our Captain the Lord's army shall march on." The congregation burst into spontaneous applause as young Michael thanked the pastor and handed back the microphone.

The visiting speaker stared in amazement. The child had actually encouraged the congregation! He had spoken with confidence and clarity. This was no game. The response of the congregation was not condescending tolerance of the child, but genuine appreciation for the Word of the Lord spoken through him. Since then, our guest minister has shared Michael's experience in places where she has traveled. She hopes that her audiences will receive faith to release their children into true usefulness and genuine ministry under the anointing of the Holy Spirit.

Michael was also a faithful prayer supporter of the pastor. His prayers were not mere religious phrases. He loved his pastor, and God gave him prayers to pray for her that would often bring comfort and encouragement, and softness to a heart threatened by hardness through pain. When the time came for Michael to move with his family to another state, he sought out his pastor. "Let me pray for you," he said. "I'll be gone a long time and

I'm so sorry to leave you." Then followed words full of love, faith, and sympathy. This time pastor and child wept together. It would be a great loss for them, for there is no more precious relationship than one established in prayer.

A Sense of Destiny Defined

Destiny, according to *Webster*, simply means "a predetermined course of events." It shares the same root word as the word *predestinate*. When our children say "yes" to God, they will receive a sense of destiny because the Word teaches "...He also did predestinate [them] to be conformed to the image of His Son..." (Rom. 8:29). That spiritual reality gives our children a desire for purpose, which we as parents need to nurture. They want to be a part of what God is doing in the earth.

Purpose differs from destiny. It means "something set up as an object or end to be attained" (Webster). God determines His purpose for everyone who has chosen to know Him (Rom. 8:28). He then takes the responsibility to follow through, after He calls us, to the end of His purpose: "...whom He called, them He also justified: and whom He justified, them He also glorified" (Rom. 8:30). Through a personal relationship with God, we discover our sense of destiny and then begin to find the purpose for which we were born.

Do we dare to believe that our children can realize this sense of destiny and begin to walk in divine purpose at such a young age as Michael? Can we expect that the promise recorded in Isaiah is meant for us?

> *For I will pour water upon him that is thirsty, and floods upon the dry ground: I will pour My spirit upon thy seed, and My blessing upon thine offspring: and they shall spring up as among the grass, as willows by the water courses. One shall say, I am the Lord's; and another shall call himself by the name of Jacob; and another shall subscribe with his hand unto the Lord, and surname himself by the name of Israel.*
>
> Isaiah 44:3-5

I believe that our only hindrance to seeing this promise fulfilled is that, as parents and leaders, we lack a sense of destiny for our children. Many times our expectation has been that *someday*, or when they become a certain age, our children will serve the Lord. Is it possible that our children and youth have not seen themselves as the Church of today because we have called them the Church of *tomorrow*? For example, in times of worship and training, many churches have either removed children to a setting "on their level" or relegated them to a spectator status among us. Obviously, some training on their level is beneficial. Isolating them from adult worship, however, prohibits their exposure to proper role models that could be their guide to worshiping God.

Role Models

The Scriptures give beautiful examples of children who learned to worship God and minister unto the Lord, fulfilling God's purpose for their lives. Samuel was only a child when he began to minister unto the Lord (see 1 Sam. 3). The Lord began to speak to Samuel, and Eli taught him how to respond to the Lord. His ministry was before Eli, but "unto the Lord" (v. 1). The Lord spoke to Samuel, and Samuel ministered to Eli. A child spoke to a priest what God had revealed to him. The word Samuel spoke was so accurate that Eli did not doubt that it was the Word of the Lord.

Jeremiah was a prophet when he was still a teenager. When he protested to the Lord that he was only a child, the Lord told him not to be concerned about his age, but simply to speak what He would give him to say (see Jer. 1:6,7). Joseph, too, was a teenager when God gave him the dream of his destiny. Though his brothers did not receive the dream with great rejoicing, God eventually brought it to pass just as He had revealed it (see Gen. 37:5-8). Joseph's thoughts must have returned many times to God's promise as the years seemed to mock the possibility of the fulfillment of his dream. Yet there was a vision, a sense of destiny that shaped his life.

He knew he would not be like other boys, not even like his brothers. That *knowing* kept him faithful through temptations and snares. Neither Potiphar's wife nor prison's confinement distracted him from living to fulfill God's purpose for his life.

Contemporary Models

Considering Church history during the last three hundred years, we can cite many examples of youth who had powerful ministries. Charles Spurgeon was preaching when he was a teenager and was pastoring a large church when he was 23 years old. He spent his youth studying and preparing for the ministry God had called him to fulfill.

During the 100 years from 1762 to 1862, Wales experienced 15 great revivals. Amazingly, the Welsh children played a leading part in bringing revival to many communities. Many between 10 to 14 years of age gathered for prayer meetings together. One interesting incident is told of some of these children praying fervently for an 84-year-old man known as Old Aberleri. Shortly after that he came to the Lord. An illiterate, Old Aberleri employed the children to read the Bible to him for a half-penny per chapter.

The great Welsh revival of the early 1900's was led by Evan Roberts when he was only 21. The group who traveled with him to sing and pray were teenagers. History proves that sixteen years of age is not too young to find real usefulness in God. Rowland Jones, the famous Welsh revival preacher, and Anna Nitchmann, a teenage elder in the Moravian Church, both began their spiritual careers at this tender age.

During a revival in our church in 1980, it was very common for a young child to read a passage of Scripture as a basis for his prayer and then "pray on that Word" with fervency and faith. Because some of them had such soft voices, a parent would often say, "I'd like to make space for Mary to pray." Everyone would sit quietly for a moment to listen to the child's prayer. In this way children could be a real part of the prayer meeting.

Young people who have been used of God throughout history have had one thing in common—their parents and others imparted an atmosphere of faith and expectancy that helped to prepare them for usefulness in God. They had a sense of destiny. As children, they were prepared for God's purpose upon their lives. They were not waiting for *someday* when they would be old enough to serve God. Their parents' intention could be compared with Hannah's dedication of Samuel: "...as long as he liveth he shall be lent to the Lord..." (1 Sam. 1:28).

Our children can be affirmed and accepted as functioning parts of the Body of Christ. It is not a dream; it is the biblical pattern for children to learn to walk in the ways of God. The Holy Spirit, who is alive and at work in the lives of parents, is the same Holy Spirit who is at work in the lives of believing children. God will use them, not someday—but *now*!

The Power of Purpose

The most thrilling discovery on earth is to find out the reason for our birth. Can life possibly have meaning until this understanding comes to us? Above all else your child needs to know that he is not an accident. He is not just the product of his parents' love, or simply the result of their desire to have a child. God has a set purpose for him to be on the earth at this time.

Purpose means "original intention." God created your child with a divine purpose for him. Your child was in the mind of God from eternity, before you were ever born. Therefore, God has an original intention for every person who has ever been born. The Bible teaches this wonderful reality:

> *According as He hath chosen us in Him before the foundation of the world, that we should be holy and without blame before Him in love: having predestinated us unto the adoption of children by Jesus Christ....*
>
> Ephesians 1:4-5

Paul specifically stated what his divine purpose was. God appointed him to be a preacher, an apostle, and a teacher (see 2 Tim. 1:11). Jeremiah was called from the womb, and was ordained of God a prophet to the nations (see Jer. 1:5). The Psalmist declared of God, "For Thou didst form my inward parts; Thou didst weave me in my mother's womb" (Ps. 139:13 NAS). And he understood that all the days ordained for him were written in God's book "when as yet there was not one of them" (Ps. 139:16 NAS).

To "Train up a child in the way he should go" (Prov. 22:6a) is to train him in the way of God's purpose, His original intention for him. The Hebrew word *derek*, translated "way," literally means "a course of life or journey." We can only find our course of life as we find the purpose of God for our lives. And we can never expect to be fulfilled in life unless we know the purpose for which we were born. The Creator Himself has established His purpose for every life. Without finding that divine purpose, our lives are doomed to meaningless futility.

Creature Abuse

Not only has God created us with a purpose, He has also given us a guidebook, His written Word, to show us how we should function in life. The Bible contains all the principles necessary for living life successfully in accordance with His plan for us. I like what Myles Munroe has said about the importance of knowing that we are created with a purpose. He explains that failure to understand the intention for any created product results in abuse. Anything of value that is manufactured always comes with a manual that explains its purpose and proper use and gives warnings against misuse. So God has given His creation a manual to follow so that they do not abuse themselves or one another.[1]

If a man does not understand God's purpose for marriage, for example, he will abuse the covenant he makes with his wife by committing adultery, or otherwise abusing his wife emotionally or physically. In that same way, not understanding God's plan for a healthy body will cause us to abuse our bodies through neglect, or by taking in harmful substances. And if a child does not understand God's purpose for his life, he will abuse the opportunity he has to receive training for that purpose.

Many young lives of children and teenagers are wasted on the things of the world that dull and damage them. That is abuse. If a parent uses his child's life to vicariously live out his unfulfilled desires of what he never achieved, he is abusing the child. That child will not be able to find the purpose of God for his life. Wherever there is a lack of understanding of divine purpose there will necessarily be abuse.

Evolutionary theories have left children feeling rudderless. Without a starting point, they are doomed to live lives of obscurity that will end in oblivion. Nothing gives meaning to life like knowing that the Creator of the universe has made you with a specific purpose for your life. Children who understand what God is doing in the earth today are greatly privileged. Their lives are not depressing and meaningless as are the lives of so many of their peers. They have found the meaning of life in God and His purpose.

Notes

1. Myles Munroe, *Pursuit of Purpose*, (Shippensburg, PA., Destiny Image, 1992), p. 32.

Chapter 2

The Joshua Generation

God is ministering to and dealing with children and teenagers in a very special way today. He is drawing the hearts of those who have given Him their lives to eternal realities, and is gifting them to fulfill their destiny as a part of God's purpose in the earth. The Joshua Generation is going to possess the promises of God in our day as young Joshua did when he led the second generation of Israelites to conquer the promised land in his day. Though the first generation who left Egypt died in the wilderness because of their unbelief, their children followed Joshua into the promised land and conquered the enemies that lived there. They received the inheritance that God had promised to give His people, a land flowing with milk and honey. This biblical type teaches us that God wants His people to conquer their enemies—the world, the flesh, and the devil—and to become the glorious Church in the earth that God has ordained (see Eph. 5:27). He wants their lives to be filled with purpose, loving Him and one another, peaceful and holy, successful and happy.

The Church will become a powerful demonstration of the love of God in the world as we follow our heavenly Joshua, as we are transformed into His image, and as we show His love to the world. For that to become a reality, the Church needs a fresh outpouring of the Holy Spirit in revival. Prophetic voices have declared that teenagers will be the backbone of the coming great flood of revival in which thousands of men and women will turn to God.

Teenagers are not going to be used by God on the strength of those prophetic words alone, however. The only way for any of us to ultimately be used by God is to personally *choose* to give our lives to God. He will use those who say "yes" to His purposes and who put themselves in a place of training and submission to the will of God. To be a part of the Joshua Generation, parents and children alike must first understand the purposes of God for this generation, and then make themselves available to God for those purposes.

A few years ago the Lord stirred my heart about our children and young people. I began an intense study of historical Christian movements in which the children followed in the footsteps of their parents. I didn't take time to study the failures. I studied those who succeeded in influencing their children, drawing them in and training them in such a way that it became the children's desire to follow God in the way their parents had served Him.

My study revealed that the Moravians were one such successful movement. I visited the Moravian villages in the eastern United States and spent several days in their libraries and archives studying their lives. They accomplished more in twenty years of involvement in foreign missions than all the other evangelical missions before them had accomplished in two hundred years. And their children continued their successful mission endeavors, sacrificing their lives as their parents had in order to follow the vision their parents had given them. My purpose in studying the Moravians was to discover the key to what they taught and how they lived that inspired a second generation to follow in their footsteps.

During the next few years, as I continued my study, I wrote two college courses for our Bible School on the subject of "Family Life and Childrearing." Since that time, we have continued to teach, through seminars, the principles we learned for training our children in the ways of God and motivating them to establish God's purposes in the earth. For many years we have given these basic principles to parents who have applied them successfully to many young lives that are now bearing fruit in His kingdom.

God's Purpose for the Family

The most important of these principles is this: *The family succeeds only to the extent that it embraces and pursues God's purpose for life.* It is natural, when we are first born again into the family of God, to expect that God is there to help us with *our* purpose. But as we grow in our knowledge of God, we realize that His Word teaches us that it is not for our purpose, but for His will and purpose that we were created.

Many unhappy families have not succeeded because they tried to add God into their own programs. They wanted Jesus to help keep their kids off drugs or away from promiscuous sex and from committing suicide. But otherwise, they wanted to live life as they desired, not considering the will of God. Many people have just wanted to have good kids who avoid destructive life styles. God began to show us that having good kids is not His purpose for their lives. The hurtful life styles of the world are just obstacles that must be removed in order to realize the eternal purpose God has for us and for our children.

A Godly Seed

The purpose of God for the family is not simply to have a successful family that doesn't end in divorce or suffer the pangs of children going into rebellion. Neither is His purpose that we be seen as happy people who are attentive to one another. God's purpose is not even that the whole church or community see that we are rearing "model children."

The Scriptures clearly teach the purpose of God for family:

> *And did not He make one? Yet had He the residue of the spirit. And wherefore one? That He might seek a godly seed. Therefore take heed to your spirit, and let none deal treacherously against the wife of his youth.*
>
> Malachi 2:15

God's stated purpose for our children is that they be a godly seed who love and glorify Him. That is why He made marriage. It was not merely to fulfill our own desires, nor to give us children just because we want the experience of childbearing or want to be admired by family members and friends. God's purpose was to produce a godly seed.

When God created Adam and Eve He blessed them and told them to be fruitful and multiply. God's desire was to have a family with whom He could share His love. Though He knew Adam would fail, He had already planned the remedy for that failure through the godly seed of His Son. He made it possible for us to fulfill the purpose of God by having a godly seed in the earth to share His love and holiness.

The Scriptures teach that as Christians we are not our own; we have been bought with a price and our responsibility is to glorify God in our body (see 1 Cor. 6:20). Knowing this, we can be free from a performance mentality that seeks the approval of other parents or relatives. Instead of being good in peoples' eyes, we will try to be godly in all we do. If we train our children with this understanding, they can be spared the enslavement to futile drives and ambitions that waste the lives of so many young people. It is a tremendous freedom to know that you are rearing your children for God's purpose and not your own, your children's, or society's.

Goals That Fulfill Purpose

What is the use of speaking about the Joshua Generation of today that will enter into a godly inheritance, if we send our children out with worldly priorities as the goal for their lives? Getting an education, marrying, and having a family are legitimate goals, but they are not the ultimate purpose for life. These are provisions of God, but they should never be confused with His ultimate purpose. Making these goals the priority of life will thwart the larger purpose of God.

Some young people marry too soon or marry the wrong person because their goal in life was simply to get married. They did not consider the purpose of God, seeking His Kingdom first and seeing these things added in God's time and way as He has promised (see Mt. 6:33). Even the wonderful hope of marriage must be submitted to the will of God or the results will be disastrous.

Other young people become hopelessly absorbed in the pursuit of a career, forgetting to seek God to know His purpose for their lives. God expects us to work and to pursue a valid way of making a living. It is God's desire to reward us for our labor and to give us increase in material ways. The Book of Proverbs is replete with instructions about how He plans to do this. But young people should not be encouraged to make their vocation the priority of their life. We need to make a living, but we don't have to lose God's purpose for our lives in the process. Personal goals must be prayerfully submitted to the will of God in order for us to be able to fulfill the purpose of God for our lives.

His Objective or Ours?

Perhaps in your early catechism you learned that "the chief end of man is to enjoy God and glorify Him." It is elementary to our concepts of Christianity that man's purpose is to glorify God; that we were created for the praise of His glory. But we have been greatly influenced in the Church by society and by "Christian humanism," which makes us lose sight of that purpose and yield to the pressure of immediate gratification. Self-realization has often replaced God's call to commitment and sacrifice. Failing to keep God's purpose before us, we gradually succumb to compromise and lose the edge of commitment to that one great purpose of glorifying God.

As we have seen, our purpose is to fulfill the will of God as a family. God's divine plan for the family is to train our children to that end. Joshua could say with conviction because he saw God's purpose, "As for me and my house, we will serve the Lord" (Josh. 24:15). One way to keep from being sidetracked is to ask ourselves at every step along the way: Is this unto that? Does this goal serve the will of God for our family? That, which we have acknowledged as God's purpose for our lives, must be the measuring line for every opportunity or seeming success.

It is the responsibility of parents to set the family's goals in the purpose of God. After specific goals have been established for our family, then the training of our children must be to the end of fulfilling those goals. God could make the staggering promise to Abraham that his seed would number as the stars because He knew Abraham's commitment to the purpose of God:

> [And the Lord said,] *For I know him, that he will command his children and his household after him, and they shall keep the way of the Lord, to do justice and judgment....*
>
> Genesis 18:19

Enemies to the Process

I am convinced that the greatest enemy to fulfilling the purpose of God as a family is philosophical in nature. It is not circumstances nor situations that hinder us from fulfilling the purpose of God. Our greatest hindrance is that our thinking becomes clouded with the philosophies of this world.

Secular Humanism. The philosophy or religion of humanism is the cradle of secular thought in our nation today. Though it is not our purpose here to fully explain this ungodly philosophy, we must refer to some of its basic tenants to understand how it militates against Christian philosophy. In this philosophical system endorsed by our educators, the highest goal for the individual is self-realization. This idea only reinforces the tendency in human nature to prideful self-centeredness, making it as natural as breathing. It translates personal achievement, competitive activities, and "may the best man win" attitudes as the "good things" in life. To the humanist, these are the things that form the character of the "born good" child who only needs the right opportunities to make him even better.

Christianity teaches that no one is born good, that we all must be born again, and that it is only the Christ-life lived through us that makes our lives of any real value. The humanist insists that "deep down he has a good heart," no matter how contrary the evidence of his rebellious life style is. The Bible contradicts this idea by teaching that the heart is deceitful above all things, and desperately wicked (Jer. 17:9). Secular humanism is absolutely opposed to the truth of the Word of God, denying the existence of God and man's need for Him.

"Christian" Humanism. The philosophy of humanism has accommodated itself to the teachings of the Church and is honeycombed throughout much of the training and practice in church activities and curriculum. Anything that strengthens selfishness and promotes personal goals above the purpose of God is a hindrance to the sacrificial commitment, which is our calling. Though some teaching sounds as if it will strengthen the family, in the end it weakens the family's interaction with and commitment to the Body of Christ.

For example, the concept of putting the family before the church in order of importance is a confusion of God's purpose. Though it sounds as if it will strengthen the family, it results in cultivating an attitude of selfishness in the family as it relates to the church. This ultimately causes the family to miss the mark, which is to live life for God's glory.

It is our responsibility to find the will of God for our lives within God's eternal purpose. The Scriptures clearly teach God's divine purpose for us:

> *According as He hath chosen us in Him before the foundation of the world, that we should be holy and without blame before Him in love: having predestinated us unto the adoption of children by Jesus Christ to Himself, according to the good pleasure of His will ... that we should be to the praise of His glory....*
>
> Ephesians 1:4-5,12

When we are born again we enter God's family, the household of faith. We cannot separate God's family from our earthly family because the Church, God's family, is made up of our earthly families. So we do not go to church, we are the Church. And the Church functions as successfully as our families function. If we are dedicated to God's purpose of living holy lives before Him in love, and of becoming mature sons of God that bring Him glory in the earth, the Church will function as the glorious Church that God intends it to be. We will be cleansed of the humanistic desire for self-realization as we realize the purpose of God for our lives.

Unbiblical Priorities

Sometimes people have difficulty deciding right priorities for the family. There does not need to be any strife or frustration in this matter of setting priorities. The godly pattern for living follows God's eternal purpose as revealed in the Scriptures. If we set God's purpose first in our lives, we will see clearly how all other goals fit into that purpose. That is why Jesus taught us to seek His Kingdom first.

For example, if there doesn't seem to be any time to give to the vision of our local church that represents God's purpose for us, we need to narrow our involvements and interests outside that vision. Some of these other activities may not be wrong in themselves, but they do nothing to build the inner man of the spirit where the life of God dwells. Remember, the world has nothing to contribute to your inner man. That's why Jesus asked the awful question, "For what shall it profit a man, if he shall gain the whole world, and lose his own soul?" (Mk. 8:36).

Our society has offered so many attractive things for our children and teenagers that many times parents have involved them in activities to the point that they have become a burden rather than a help in their development. But we can deliberately choose to simplify our life styles and narrow our involvements. And we will find a wonderful freedom when we do.

A Selfish Home Spirit

William Booth, the founder of the Salvation Army, listed one of the hindrances to training children to have a part in the Kingdom, as a selfish home spirit. This is the mentality that believes the family exists as an end in itself. Booth said that to be godly, every home must be hospitable to those without and must share the members of their family to accomplish the work of God. We cannot be a part of God's plan to redeem mankind unless we include goals outside the home that effect that plan.[1]

The teenagers in our church, from the time they were small children, have been happily involved in the activities and ministries of the church as a way of life, not as an added enrichment. Their parents never taught them that they could have other priorities above attending church services or prayer meetings. They have always felt accepted as a valuable functioning part of the Body of Christ, the family of God. They believe that they are a vital part of a wonderful, exciting thing that God is doing in the earth; not that they have some duty to fulfill to attend church. The maxim is true that says, "As a twig is bent, so grows the tree."

Formula for Success

We have had twenty years to observe the outworking of the principles we have taught in the area of childrearing and we have seen many young lives transformed during this time. They have been trained in our Christian Academy, our Bible School, and in our church classes. And we have continually taught our parents the biblical principles for godly homes. Those parents who have been successful in raising a godly seed have laid hold of three keys:

(1) *They believed the teaching.*

(2) *They practiced what they were taught.*

(3) *They trained their children in the way that was taught.*

Unfortunately we have also observed some failures. We have found that they are usually the result of two things:

(1) *A duplicitous attitude that is not supportive of the full program of teaching,*

(2) *A legalistic attitude that declares "the pastor says," rather than lovingly training the child from their own conviction of what has been taught.*

Will your children be a part of the Joshua Generation? Will they know the success that comes only from finding their purpose in life as they fulfill the goals that God has ordained for them? How you, as a parent, respond to the purpose of God will directly affect your children's lives. It is never too soon to begin to seek God for His eternal purpose to be revealed to them.

Notes

1. Booth, William, *Training of Children,* (Salem, Ohio: Schmul Publications., 1984 ed.), p. 50.

Chapter 3

It's Never Too Soon

When the Lord placed His specific call for service on the lives of children in the Bible, He first sent a message to the parents of that child. He helped the parents to understand that the destiny of their child was to be committed to His plan, but the rearing of the child was their responsibility as godly parents.

Consecration from the Womb

One biblical example of this truth was when an angel visited the parents of Samson to tell them what kind of upbringing they should provide for their son because God had chosen him to be a deliverer for Israel. He specifically told them that

Samson was to drink no wine or strong drink, nor to eat any unclean thing; his hair was not to be cut with a razor. The angel instructed Samson's parents that he was to be "a Nazarite unto God from the womb" (Judg. 13:4-5). Unfortunately, parents today often wait too late to begin the prayerful preparation of their children for God's purpose upon their lives. God's preparation begins from the womb.

Samson is not the only example of children being consecrated from the womb. The word of the Lord concerning Jeremiah was "...before thou camest forth out of the womb I sanctified thee, and I ordained thee a prophet unto the nations" (Jer. 1:5). John the Baptist could go on record as the youngest child ever filled with the Holy Spirit. Not only was he filled with the Spirit from his mother's womb (see Lk. 1:15), but in the womb he leaped for joy at the salutation of Mary, the mother of Jesus (Lk. 1:44). Even before conception there should be prayerful dedication of the expected child. Hannah gave herself to God in prayer before the conception of Samuel. This prepared her heart to give him up fully to the purpose of God (1 Sam. 1:27-28).

The apostle Paul wrote of the influence of parents and grandparents in the preparation of young Timothy's life and attitudes. He declared that the faith that was in Timothy "dwelt first in thy grandmother Lois, and thy mother Eunice" (2 Tim. 1:5). How important it is for parents to realize they can impart faith in God to their children!

Obviously, God can and does call those who have had an improper or even heathenistic background. The process that I have outlined of God instructing parents and parents responding to God before the conception of their children is not a law. But it is a valuable principle as seen in the pattern of Scripture and life. It reflects the responsibility that parents have to train their children in the ways of God. The promise to those who "train up a child in the way he should go" is that "when he is old, he will not depart from it" (Prov. 22:6). That promise is also a principle that can be applied for anticipated results. It defines the call of God upon every parent's life to train his children.

Pervasive Training

John the Baptist was born to parents who were "both righteous before God, walking in all the commandments" (Lk. 1:6). John's life style with godly parents provided the atmosphere for his preparation to serve God and helped him to conform to God's purposes. His father, Zechariah, was executing his office as priest, burning incense in the temple when the angel of the Lord appeared to him to announce John's birth. Zechariah and Elizabeth had already established a life of obedience and worship in their home. Love and service to the Lord must have pervaded all that was said and done in their godly lives.

The Scriptures give explicit instructions for parents to maintain the spiritual atmosphere in which to nurture a child. In the Book of Deuteronomy, parents are instructed to teach their children diligently in the ways of God:

> *And thou shalt teach them* [My words] *diligently unto thy children, and thou shalt talk of them when thou sittest in thine house, and when thou walkest by the way, and when thou liest down, and when thou risest up.*
>
> Deuteronomy 6:7

To teach children diligently is a challenge that many young parents are not prepared for. The parent who teaches his children diligently will find that he must discipline himself before he can discipline his children. In every area of life, order and discipline must be applied to be sure we will realize the purpose of God for our children.

"When thou sittest in thine house." How much time is spent *watching* rather than *talking* when we sit at leisure in our homes? Zig Ziglar teaches, in his book, *Raising Positive Kids In A Negative World,* that every hour of staring at television is one less hour invested in personal motivation, mental creativity, and actual involvement in the lives of others.[1] The intrusion of sights and sounds through electronic devices can displace the once-common art of talking.

The problem is that so much of what our children hear does not instruct them in the "way they should go." They are receiving instruction, however, and being influenced in their thinking because they are listening to *someone* who is talking. According to the Scriptures, that someone should be the parent. We can out-talk the world. We can out-talk the devil. It is not only a matter of giving our children our personal input; it is vital that we do not leave a place for the wrong input.

"When thou walkest by the way." This refers to the activities of life that are a part of our daily involvements. My mother used any occasion as an opportunity to instruct me. I remember her saying, "Go ask your daddy if you can go—and hold your shoulders up."

And at the dinner table,

"Sue, pass the potatoes, please—and smile."

If I spoke too loudly in a group of people, I would hear Mother's patient voice, "Don't draw attention to yourself; it isn't ladylike."

Continuing instruction as we "walk by the way" can be a pleasure to our children if done in a kind and respectful manner. Children like to know that parents are aware of them. Many little hearts are aching for the affectionate sound of their parent's voice. Adults who are always making a bid for attention are most often those who were neglected when they were children. Instructing our children reassures them of our love and concern for them.

"When thou liest down." Here is another opportunity to teach our children. One man told me that he realized how much his child wanted to talk with him when it was time to go to bed. At other times he had tried to open conversations with his son without success. So he began putting him to bed 20 minutes early to give time for a bedtime talk. For many families, children's bedtime is the only good time to teach them the Bible or read them stories. It is a great time to pray, helping the children to get rid of the frustrations of the day or to prepare for the next day.

"And when thou risest up." Every morning presents us another day that we can continue to guide our children. If a child forms a lifelong habit of morning prayer, he is not likely to break the pattern as an adult. A good level of discipline is required to sustain this habit, but the rewards are wonderful. It doesn't take long to read a few verses of Scripture at the breakfast table and to pray with our little ones before they leave for school. This sets a tone for the day and reminds our children again of the Lordship of Jesus in their lives.

First Impressions Count

Comenius, one of the world's great educators, had an understanding of the importance of molding and training children from their infancy. He expressed his conviction in this way: "It is eternal truth that first impressions adhere most firmly to our minds. Whatever first attaches to children at this tender age, whether good or bad, cleaves to them deepest as long as they live and cannot be expelled by any after impressions."[2]

We have learned much through extensive studies about the early, impressionable years in a child's life. Still, too often, parents do not assume the responsibility to provide an atmosphere conducive to their children's experiencing the right impressions in a consistent way. I once heard an evangelist with a very great ministry give credit to his parents for doing this very thing. He said, "Jesus was always the unseen guest in our home. My parents both talked about Him and to Him."

The parent will succeed who sincerely seeks the answer to the question that Samson's father asked, "How shall we order the child, and how shall we do unto him?" (See Judges 13:12.) Parents have asked the "experts" how to rear children, and they have asked other parents. But it is when they begin to ask the Lord how to order their children's lives that the purpose of producing a godly seed will be realized. And only then, as attention is given to carry out God's instructions diligently, can we expect to enjoy godly children.

The School of Infancy

Do we realize that from the time our children are infants the training process begins? Why did Samson's parents ask the angel, "How shall we order the child's life?" I believe they knew that they needed retraining from the world's methods of childrearing. They could not assume that a child dedicated to God's purpose could be reared according to the pattern of their day.

Our society has been so deluged with psychological approaches, and has become so fascinated with any new idea, that the result has been absolute confusion. Since Dr. Spock has apologized, and the teachings of others have had time to run their course with unsuccessful results, the light is beginning to dawn for many that there is truth in God's Word, after all, regarding the training of children. The Scriptures are full of instruction concerning how to rear children. The Book of Proverbs, especially, teaches parents about children, and warns them of the grief and disappointment that will come to parents who disregard the necessity of vigilant parenting.

Practical Considerations

In my studies of successful Christian parents in history, I observed some of the practical considerations for rearing children that they had learned.

Through waiting on God, without the help of psychologists, they discovered ways to meet the needs of their children.

Susannah Wesley, who raised ten children to serve God effectively, realized that infants and little children need a regular schedule in order to feel secure. She maintained a strict order in her home that included private time for every child to spend with her. She also taught her young children to "cry softly." This would circumvent much "tantrum" anger if taught to children today. She never caused her children to suppress laughter unless it was "unseasonable." Therefore, laughter and happiness were cultivated and positively reinforced. She also taught them to pray as infants on her knee, where they learned reverence for God and respect for adults at a very early age.

Part of the family altar time could be the reading of Christian literature and of the lives of missionaries. Singing worship songs and praise choruses can replace the music the world has to offer. Every time children sing to God, the message is written again on their own hearts.

From the Cradle

It is through God's Word that we learn that it is never too soon to begin the training of our children. When the Holy Spirit brought sovereign revival to our church a few years ago, we found ourselves in prayer meetings for hours enjoying the presence of God night and day. No one wanted to miss the wonderful things God was doing in our midst.

The young mothers did not want to be deprived of these blessings because of caring for their small children. When I went to God in prayer for guidance concerning these mothers, He showed me the Scripture, "Gather the people, sanctify the congregation, assemble the elders, **gather the children, and those that suck the breasts**" (Joel 2:16a). These instructions were specifically given by the prophet Joel for a time of revival. We had our answer. The parents brought the children, including the infants, and the Holy Spirit has taught us how to train them to be a part of our prayer meetings.

In our church we have nurseries for infants and young children especially for Sunday and midweek services, but we have encouraged our parents to bring their babies and small children to our church prayer meetings. In this way they learn how to be a part of that corporate prayer life in which their parents are involved. By the time our children are around three years old, they usually can pray aloud in a prayer meeting. They have learned that this is a part of life, just like eating and sleeping.

Although it is foreign to our American way of thinking, God's Word instructs us to train children in His ways from the time of infancy. The prophet Isaiah declared:

> *Whom shall He teach knowledge? And whom shall He make to understand doctrine? Them that are weaned from the milk, and drawn from the breasts. For precept must be upon precept, precept upon precept; line upon line, line upon line; here a little, and there a little.*
>
> Isaiah 28:9-10

It is this diligent and gradual exercise in the truth that shapes the life of the smallest child. We need to ask God for the patience to teach line upon line, precept upon precept, here a little, there a little, until our children are trained in the knowledge of God. We must win their hearts and train them God's way before the forces of the world try to train them another way. If we are faithful, our children will develop a capacity for God that cannot be satisfied with anything the world offers. They will be satisfied with our love and with their love for God. And they will be equipped to become a part of the Joshua Generation.

Notes

1. Zig Ziglar, *Raising Positive Kids in a Negative World,* (Nashville, Tennessee: Thomas Nelson, 1985), p. 116.

2. John Amos Comenius, *School of Infancy,* (Chapel Hill: University of North Carolina Press, 1956), p. 115.

Chapter 4

Winning Their Hearts

"I don't think we should *force* our children to go to church. I'm in church today because I *chose* to be. My parents never made me go to church."

The woman stood to voice her opinion as I finished my teaching session on parents' responsibility to train their children in the "way they should go." There had been no suggestion in my teaching that children should be forced, but that was the perception of this frustrated listener.

Between the two extremes of forcing our children and giving up on them, there is another way that works—winning. It is not possible to force another to believe or to have true dedication to a cause. We can only force someone to comply with laws or standards. When one is made to conform against his will, he usually does so in anger or bitterness. This is why the Scripture says, "...the law worketh wrath" (Rom. 4:15a).

Winning the Affection

I wrote earlier of my studies to discover how godly parents historically have been able to win their children to the purpose of God. Such was the success of the Moravians, that year after year found their children following in their parents' footsteps, choosing joyfully to continue the work to which their parents had given their lives. The Moravians' approach to rearing their children produced amazing fruit reflected in sterling dedication to God and missionary zeal.

A statement of their leader, Count Zinzendorf, became one of the keys that God gave me for successful childrearing—a fundamental truth that would produce a godly seed. The key, simply stated, is to *win the affection of the child.* Zinzendorf declared adamantly, "If parents who are themselves fully consecrated to the Savior can succeed in holding the affection of their children, they have already won them."[1] Winning the affections is not the only thing involved in rearing godly children, of course, but it is a vital key. We can't win our children to Jesus until we have first won their hearts to ourselves. Even if the child comes to the Lord, we cannot train him unless he knows we really love him. John Maxwell has said it well: "People don't care how much you know until they know how much you care."

There will be no progress in achieving godly goals for our children's lives until we first win their hearts to ourselves. Zinzendorf's understanding was that children should be lovingly drawn, not forced, to embrace the Christian life style.

Winning vs. Forcing

William Booth, who reared eight children to work with him in the Salvation Army, believed that parents must seek "the reign of love in their homes and make it their aim to be a mirror and foretaste of the love of heaven." I have observed that a parent who is legalistic and without love in his approach to his child will rear a hateful child. Force does not win affections. It is not force but influence that wins the child. Once the child is won, he finds happiness in fulfilling his parent's desire.

Love inspires, and inspiration is the secret of training. Force and harsh commands raise the resistance of the will, but loving influence encourages the child to "will" with the parent. In other words, you are influencing his will rather than breaking it (see Chapter 8). A child does not need to lose his will; he needs his will to be trained to choose the correct paths for his life.

In leadership training courses we teach that the highest level of authority we possess is given to us by the permission of those we lead, not by the position we hold. Authority that is given to us because we have earned the respect of those who willingly submit to us can be compared to the obedience that is inspired in our children through love. Ultimately our children must obey us; that is positional authority. However, when they obey because they love to please us, we have won their hearts.

Winning Through Loving

Occasionally I have heard someone say, "My father (or mother) never told me that he loved me." To some of us this seems unthinkable. But there are parents who simply have not developed any affectionate relationship with their children. To say, "I love you" as you look into the eyes of your child is going to require some further demonstrations. When we express love to our children, they begin to expect communication and to want it.

This whole dynamic involved in relating to a child causes some parents to guard against committing themselves fully to their children because openness requires further involvement of time and affection. And it makes us vulnerable to the pain of disappointment or possible rejection. The benefits of openness far surpass the risks, however, when we consider that there is no other way of winning our children's affections. To win them means we will need to be involved in loving the things our children love. It means having our hearts bound up with theirs; rejoicing over their triumphs and sympathizing with their failures.

The Power of Love

One of the most memorable pictures of love between a parent and a child is found in the life of John G. Paton, missionary to the New Hebrides. In his autobiography, Paton recalls the day he left home to attend college in preparation for going to the mission field. His father walked with him the first six miles. Following are a few quotes from that tender experience wherein Paton gives us a glimpse of the depth of impact a father's life can have on his son:

> My dear father's counsels and tears and heavenly conversation on that parting journey are fresh in my heart as if it had been yesterday; and tears are on my cheeks as freely now as then, whenever memory steals me away to the scene. For the last half-mile or so we walked on in almost

unbroken silence, my father, as was often his custom, carrying hat in hand, while his long flowing hair streamed down his shoulders. His lips kept moving in silent prayers for me, and his tears fell fast when our eyes met each other in looks for which all speech was vain. We halted on reaching the appointed parting place; he grasped my hand firmly for a minute in silence, and then solemnly and affectionately said, "God bless you, my son! Your father's God prosper you, and keep you from evil!"

Unable to say more, his lips kept moving in silent prayer; in tears we embraced, and parted. I ran off as fast as I could, and, when about to turn a corner in the road where he would lose sight of me, I looked back and saw him still standing with head uncovered where I had left him. Waving my hat in adieu, I was round the corner and out of sight in an instant. But my heart was too full and sore to carry me further, so I darted into the side of the road and wept for a time. Then, rising up cautiously, I climbed the dyke to see if he yet stood where I had left him, and just at that moment I caught a glimpse of him climbing the dyke and looking out for me! He did not see me, and after he had gazed eagerly in my direction for a while, he got down, turned his face towards home, and began to return—his head still uncovered, and his heart, I felt sure, still rising in prayers for me.

I watched through blinding tears, 'til his form faded from my gaze; and then, hastening on my way, vowed deeply and oft, by the help of God, to live and act so as never to grieve or dishonor such a father and mother as He had given me. The appearance of my father, when we parted, his advice, prayers and tears, the road, the dyke, the climbing up on it and then walking away, head uncovered, have often, often, all through life, risen vividly before my mind. In my earlier years particularly, when exposed to many temptations, his parting form rose before me as that of a guardian angel. The memory of that scene not only helped, by God's grace, to keep me pure from the prevailing sins, but also stimulated me in all my studies, that I might not fall short of his hopes, and in all my Christian duties, that I might faithfully follow his shining example.[2]

Unconditional Love

There is no other true pattern for a picture of godly love than that found in the Scriptures. Paul's classic "love chapter" (1 Cor. 13) describes the attitudes and actions of godly love. This is what the Bible refers to as *agape,* the Greek word for the highest kind of love, God's love. We can only cultivate that kind of love based on our choices, not our feelings. We must allow the Holy Spirit to shed the love of God abroad in our hearts (see Rom. 5:5) as we choose to love unconditionally. Obviously every other kind of love is conditional and based on reciprocity.

As we choose to love our children unconditionally, we will begin to show them true affection in many ways. To express love to our children the most important elements are eye contact, physical contact, and focused attention. These expressions are natural when love is flowing. If we do not feel these impulses, we should practice them in order to break down the reserve of our unaffectionate personalities.

Some parents determine to be friends with their children, rather than taking a place of authority as a parent. It is good to be a friend to them, but they need much more than the "pal" relationship if they are to live godly lives. They need love motivated by the Spirit, which is always unconditional and pure in motive, though it will sometimes need to be corrective.

It is wonderful to know that God knows we do not have this ability to love in ourselves. That is why He made a provision for this need for a pure love by giving us the Holy Spirit. Once, when "my" love had run out, the Lord allowed me to see that He had provided a source of unconditional love that never ends. It is supernatural. It is the provision of God. We receive it by asking for fresh infillings of the Holy Spirit, who, when He comes, brings an outpouring of the Father's love to our hearts.

The great love that John Paton's father showed to all of his 11 children came from his relationship with God as revealed by his marvelous prayer life. Paton said of his father's prayers,

> How much my father's prayers impressed me I can never explain, nor could any stranger understand. When, on his knees and all of us kneeling around him in family worship, he poured out his whole soul with tears for the conversion of the heathen...and for every personal and domestic need, we all felt in the presence of the living Savior, and learned to know and love Him as our Divine Friend. As we rose from our knees, I used to look at the light on my father's face, and wish I were like him in spirit...hoping that in answer to his prayers, I might be privileged and prepared to carry the blessed Gospel to some portion of the heathen world.[3]

The power of love to win and to lead is seen so clearly in this family. The example of parents' relationship with God, the power of the Holy Spirit, the tenderness of relationship—these are the things that win our children's hearts. And if we win their hearts, they will follow in our footsteps. To them it will simply be a matter of doing what comes naturally.

Notes

1. Count Zinzendorf, *Articles on Children,* (Old Salem, North Carolina, Moravian library), translated from German.

2. John G. Paton, *Missionary To The New Hebrides, An Autobiography,* (New York: Fleming H. Revell Co., 1898), pp. 40-42.

3. Ibid., pp. 20-21.

Chapter 5

Doing What Comes Naturally

What thought entered your mind when you read the title of this chapter? Probably that this chapter would address the problem of children's mischievous behavior, right? Isn't that what children *naturally* do? If we believe that, it is because we have been schooled to believe that children have a natural propensity for that which is negative or rebellious.

Obviously, everyone is born with the Adamic nature, which has a selfish bent. It is a sinful nature and must be redeemed by accepting the sacrifice of Jesus' blood. We understand that only through the born-again experience can we be free from our sinful nature. That is what Calvary is all about. However, Jesus sheds wonderful and encouraging light on the subject of a child's nature that can help us know how to train our children and bring them into the Kingdom of God.

The Kingdom Nature

In Jesus' teaching, He opens for us the understanding that for one to be converted, he must become as a little child (see Mt. 18:1-5). Jesus showed that a little child is a picture of the Kingdom nature. The identifying characteristic of child-likeness is humility (Mt. 18:4). Jesus told His disciples that they could not even enter the Kingdom unless they became as these little children. He was, thereby, teaching them that the Kingdom of God belongs to children as well as to adults.

The significance of what Jesus was saying was that adults must learn to respond as children do in order to have a part in the Kingdom. That presents to us the question, "How do little children respond?" They are naturally trusting, loving, and forgiving, desiring to please those they love. Because of these natural responses, children feel at home in the Kingdom reality where the love of God is manifest.

Though kids may not always *tell* the truth, they *like* the truth. They feel secure when people tell them the truth. They like it more than adults do sometimes. A mother in our congregation was endeavoring to console her four-year-old son, Stephen, who had a strong disagreement with his little friend. In the end, her son's friend had yelled at him that he never wanted to be his friend again. This scenario was repeated several times.

One day Stephen came home very upset because his friend had yelled at him one more time. His mother, in exasperation said, "Look, Stephen, why don't you just go play by yourself or find yourself another friend?" Stephen responded, "Oh I can't do that. I have to forgive him. I forgive him all the time." It was more natural for Stephen to forgive 70 times 7, as Jesus taught we should do, than it was for his mother. He was simply applying the truth he had learned.

Kids get frustrated with hypocrisy. There is something in their nature that will respond positively to truth and to a life that is lived according to the will of God. They are easily inspired to accept a challenge that is beyond themselves. Their faith is uncomplicated. They have not yet woven a protective web of excuses to shield them from the necessity of responding to the truth.

Let Them Come to Me

Children respond easily to the truth of the gospel. It is not a matter of parents having to drive or force children to Jesus. Jesus said to the disciples, "Let them come to Me; do not hinder them" (see Mk. 10:14). They wanted to come to Jesus; it was the disciples who were hindering them.

Again Jesus said, "For of such is the kingdom of God" (see Mk. 10:14b). He was perturbed that the disciples did not understand the importance of children having the liberty to come to Him. It has been my experience that children love who Jesus is. They love His Kingdom purpose and love being a part of something miraculous and eternal.

As I have challenged our young people to allow the Lord to use them in prophecy, in witnessing, in praying, and in bringing souls to the Lord, I have seen a real desire in their hearts for those things. Of course, they can be tempted by the things of the world. So can we. But it is not true that they would rather waste their time on the things of the world. They have a desire to be useful in the things of the Kingdom of God. That desire simply needs to be recognized and nurtured.

We say that the world has a real pull on our children. That is true mainly *because they have so much exposure to worldly things, not because it is inherent in their nature.* The more they are exposed to worldly influences, the more their spirits are hardened by them. But if we minister the love and life of the Kingdom to them, they are drawn into the Kingdom of God. The world has a pull on our children only after we initiate (or allow) the opportunities for such involvements, not before.

Children are like wet cement waiting for the imprint of the exposure we allow. Those who watch violent TV programming will be rambunctious and tend to re-enact what they have seen. Children who listen to hard rock music with its rebellious and sex-oriented lyrics will become rebellious, dark, and preoccupied with sex. It is equally true that children who spend time in prayer, worship, and edifying conversation will reflect that involvement in their attitudes and pursuits. Parents are responsible to let their children come to Jesus and not be hindered by worldly attractions.

Kingdom Blessing

Jesus' response to the desire of children to come to Him was that He "took them up in His arms, put His hands upon them, and blessed them" (Mk. 10:16). This is a marvelous demonstration of Jesus' love and acceptance. The blessing of the Lord does not come upon materialistic things, upon that which pride builds, or on that from which we draw our own accolades. When the Lord Jesus begins blessing people, their blessing is eternal, though sometimes it is not the kind of blessing we are looking for.

Divine Blessing

In the beatitudes, Jesus surprises us by telling us which people are blessed—the poor in spirit, the peacemakers (see Mt. 5:3,9). We often endeavor to bless our children in our own way. We arrange life around them and set up a future for them, and try to insulate them from the dealings of God that, if allowed, would build godly character.

God's blessing is the blessing our children need. The Scriptures teach that "The blessing of the Lord, it maketh rich, and He addeth no sorrow with it" (Prov. 10:22). When we bless our children and teenagers in our shallowness and shortsightedness, we sometimes deprive them of the true blessing of God. Our kind of blessing often produces the ungrateful child who "has everything" and after opening dozens of Christmas presents, looks around and says, "Is that all?"

God's blessing does not promote selfishness, but brings eternal satisfaction. God is going to bless some of our children by sending them to the nations to share Jesus with other peoples. Some will minister in this nation and in their local community. It is beyond our imagining how God may use our children if they continue in the blessing of the Lord.

The Joshua Generation will know that the blessing of the Lord is of far greater benefit than the natural experiences and material things of this life.

God will reveal to them the "pearl of great price." For joy, they will be willing, as was the man in Jesus' parable, to sell their entanglements with this world and become a part of God's great purpose (see Mt. 13:46).

We will need to be careful when we see them wanting to sell all they have to "buy the field" where the treasure is, that we not hinder them through our ideals of security and respectability in life. We will need to give them room to place a greater value on this divine blessing than we have. The Scriptures say that the man sold all he had for joy of finding such a treasure (Mt. 13:44). In spite of the fact that suicide is a leading cause of death today among American teenagers, there will be a Joshua generation of young people that will demonstrate the joy of discovering the great treasure of life. For joy they will sell all and buy the treasure of loving and serving Jesus and being a part of His great purpose in the earth.

Parental Blessing

There is a godly parental blessing that we can give to our children. The authors of *The Blessing,* a study of the biblical patriarchal blessing, tell us that the literal meaning of the word *blessing* in Hebrew is "to bow the knee." It is a word used to show reverence or awe to a person and carries the undertanding that if I have blessed a person, I have placed a high value on that person.[1]

Our children first of all need Jesus' blessing; then they need their parents' blessing. The patriarchal blessing involved:

(1) meaningful touch,

(2) a spoken message,

(3) attaching high value to the one being blessed,

(4) picturing a special future for them,

(5) and making an active commitment to fulfill the blessing given.[2]

This kind of personal affirmation is what God intended for us to give our children. I believe that the Lord wants to anoint us so we can bless with the blessing with which He blesses.

Kingdom Demonstration

The Bible teaches that Jesus will establish a Millennial Kingdom here on this earth after His return, during which all will live in peace and will love each other (see Zech. 8). That is the context of the Old Testament Scriptures that speak of the consummation of the Kingdom. As Christians, we look forward with anticipation to God's Kingdom of love and peace ruling the earth. However, everywhere that we are able to give demonstrations presently of

God's Kingdom reality, purpose, and life style, we are saying to those around us: "the kingdom of God has come unto you" (Mt. 12:28). We can have manifestations of the Kingdom of peace and love on earth before the final fulfillment of God's Word.

From the time Jesus came to this earth and started healing the sick and saying "the kingdom of heaven is at hand" (Mt. 4:17), His intention was that we give present Kingdom demonstration and manifestation through our lives, through our ministry, and in our interaction with people. We are to show people what the Kingdom of God's love is going to be like when it is fully consummated.

In the biblical description of the Millenial Kingdom we see children at play and living in safety. "And the streets of the city shall be full of boys and girls playing in the streets thereof" (Zech. 8:5). What a lovely description of the Kingdom of God! One picture of the Millenial Kingdom says that children will play on the hole of an asp without harm, the lamb and lion will lie down together, and nothing shall hurt anything on God's holy mountain (see Is. 11:8-9). The millennial reign of Jesus will be a time of absolute preservation and safety, and none shall be harmed or hurt, defiled or destroyed.

Preservation

As we have seen, the Bible shows us the characteristics of life lived in the Kingdom of God. In the consummation of God's Kingdom here on earth, nothing shall hurt the children physically, mentally, or spiritually. Every contrary force will be at peace with the other. In that day the bells of the horses and every pot will have written on it, "Holiness unto the Lord" (Zech. 14:20). The understanding is that everything in the world of commerce is going to have written on it, "Holiness unto the Lord."

No unholy thing will be allowed to tempt or destroy anyone through greed or other evil motives. This Millenial Kingdom is going to be a glorious place to live! It will be a place fit for children—and a place fit for children is fit for adults. Where a child is safe, everyone is safe. You may be wondering at this point what this Millenial Kingdom picture has to do with the kids of the Kingdom now. Just this:

Safety

The measure in which our children are presently safe from the powers of evil is the measure in which we have allowed God's Kingdom to come on the earth in our lives. The humanist wants to oppose this philosophy. He doesn't want your children to be safe. He wants your children to be eaten up with the doctrine of exposure. He insists that your children need to be exposed to the real world, which is his atheistic world. The humanist says we are not being realistic because we want our children to be safe from their ungodly philosophies and life styles.

The fact is, the world has defaulted in providing a proper atmosphere for children on every count. From the streets to the schools there is no safety. Satan has a counterfeit "safeness." One such counterfeit is "safe sex." How can you be safe having sex you shouldn't have? Safe sex really teaches children how to sin without contracting a fatal disease.

If we had the Kingdom of God established for our children, if it were the millenial reign of Christ, what would we have? No pornography, no drunkenness, no gambling, no violence or suicide, no vile language, no suggestive conversation on TV or in movies, no power playing, no promiscuous sex or opportunity for it, no defilement of the imagination through books or conversation.

The day is coming, when Jesus returns, that nothing will exist except His Kingdom reality. Until then, inasmuch as we establish God's Kingdom of love on the earth, we have established reality, and we will have shown people the power of God. All the evils we have mentioned are allowed in the streets of America for monetary and social gain out of a greed motive. As a nation, we have not believed the Word of the Lord that says we can establish a demonstration of God's Kingdom reality right here on earth.

When John Wesley visited the Moravians, he said that if God would have let him he would have stayed in their village the rest of his life, for he experienced

God's wonderful Kingdom of love and light there. It was a place of Kingdom reality because men, women, and children gave themselves to Kingdom realities of peace and safety and the purposes of God. Their whole life style demonstrated the reality of the Kingdom of God.

In the Millenial Kingdom, everyone will be safe. If we want to live now in the Kingdom of love and life, we must provide true safety as Jesus taught it. The world calls this safety "unreality" or "isolationism." But a casual observation of their "reality" life styles reveals that they have problems we don't want.

Kingdom blessing and Kingdom demonstration can become realities for our children as we allow the Kingdom of God to come to us and determine to *let* our children come to Jesus. They will surprise us with their willingness and understanding as we present the truth of the Kingdom to them in a loving way. They will also challenge us to become as little children, full of love and trust and a forgiving attitude, so that we can enter the Kingdom of God.

Notes

1. Gary Smalley and John Trent, *The Blessing*, (Nashville, Tennessee, Thomas Nelson Publishers, 1986), p. 26.
2. Ibid., p. 24.

Chapter 6

The Loss of Childhood

A few years ago studies revealed that children who skipped the crawling step in their development were lacking in certain motor skills. There was a problem in coordination that predicted future difficulties in learning, especially in areas of verbal mastery. Some therapists felt that the remedy lay in a restitution of that lost process, so they arranged for adult crawling sessions.

This will sound a bit ridiculous to those who have not experienced such difficulties. But my husband, John, could relate to people with verbal handicaps. As a research chemist he does very well in his field, but he cannot remember when he did not have a problem with spelling—and not a small problem. When he heard of these studies, he remembered his mother telling him that he walked when he was six months old. He never crawled. Through hard work, John overcame much of his lack in verbal ability (without crawling classes). Because of his experience we have come to appreciate the importance of the stages of childhood development. To try to restore what has been lost in a developmental gap is a very difficult task, if not an impossible one.

Psychological Gaps

It is also possible to create developmental gaps psychologically in children by failing to provide the years they need to just "be children." We would never take a high school graduate and put him in charge of a large corporation. But today's society does submit young children to knowledge and experiences that they should not have until they are teenagers or adults.

Children can tolerate and assimilate learning as it progresses through reasonable stages. However, large amounts of information, much of it in a realm beyond the child's grasp, is confusing and harmful to a child. For example, we learn about sickness, death, or sex in measured ways spaced throughout our lives. The important things of life should be told to a child at the right time by the right people.

My childhood included some years that required very little of me. That gave me an opportunity to feel safe and happy and develop some memories that comfort me even now. Some of my fondest memories involve the times I enjoyed my grandmother's wonderful gift of storytelling. Then, there were the afternoon rests lying beside my mother and planning with her what "we" would cook for supper.

Our family went to the beach together when I was 10 and my sister was 12, and we acted our age. We built sand castles and got sunburned, feeling that we were loved by our parents, who were enjoying their time with us. We were not into "preteen beautiful," or worrying about values clarification. Nobody told us anything darkly fascinating or exposed us to sights and sounds that made us feel an ashamed sense of intrigue. I thank God that, though my childhood was not perfect, I was allowed a childhood.

Great damage is done to children who are not allowed to develop naturally as children before being thrown into the adult arena of experiences and responsibilities. I am making a plea for preserving their innocence and protecting their right to mature at a proper pace. Extreme caution should be taken concerning our children's involvements and relationships.

Who Told You That You Were Naked?

The media flaunts its violent scenes and sexual involvements before the minds of children who are not emotionally or mentally prepared to handle such situations. As responsible parents, we need to counter this violation of our children by insisting that they have time for a childhood with all the privileges and experiences that should accompany it.

Today's world has been told many things that previous generations never knew, much of which they never wanted or needed to know. The information explosion has not been entirely positive, creating an inordinate lust for knowledge of all kinds. Parents are responsible to know what their child is being told and who is telling him. Good does not come from repeating sordid events in the hearing of our children. Some things that both children and adults learn or experience were never intended to intrude upon their minds and hearts.

This is why the pivotal question asked of Adam was "...Who told thee that thou wast naked? Hast thou eaten of the tree, whereof I commanded thee that thou shouldest not eat?" (Gen. 3:11) God commanded Adam not to eat of the tree of the knowledge of good and evil. When Adam and Eve disobeyed God, and ate of the forbidden tree, they realized they were naked, and they became ashamed and afraid. Until then, they were free in their innocence to walk with God and with each other, unashamed and unafraid.

Are we failing in the same way as Adam and Eve did? Are we, in our lust for knowledge, allowing our children, or ourselves, to be told things in realms that are either forbidden or untimely? I believe this is an extremely important issue to consider. I am not suggesting that we hide from truth or ignore information that is legitimate.

However, we need to determine what things are good to be exposed to and what things are to be left alone. Some realms of information are a burden to our children. When they do not understand what they are hearing or seeing, they may invent the rest of the story. Their mental and emotional development can be adversely affected through a poor understanding of inappropriate or untimely information.

As we have mentioned, films involving violence and sexual immorality are unsuitable information for children. Children can be told about society's problems by their parents at the proper time and with the right perspective. Seen as entertainment on television, these same subject areas will be improperly presented. Anger and hatred are often the motivating forces behind them.

Exposure through an "information attack," rather than learning through a timely process, is detrimental.

Every young person deserves the experience of a childhood, and childhood should last as long as we can reasonably extend it. Society is forcing children to "grow up" before they have developed an ability to deal with the experiences and problems of life at that particular level of maturity.

One excuse for wholesale exposure, at almost any age, is that we should face the reality of what life is. The argument is that it is wrong to paint a picture of life for our children that excludes violence, immorality, family breakdown, and other "normal" experiences. We must ask for wisdom to decide what experiences are normal for our children in a world that is growing more decadent each year, and endeavor to protect them from an exposure to the harshness of sin too early.

It's Okay to Be Happy

There seems to be a strange persuasion that if we face reality we must acknowledge that most families are miserable and strife-torn. Someone said concerning a television soap opera, "That's just the way life is." I asked, "Whose life? I don't know any family who has divorce, murders, and continuing intrigue on the scale of that soap-opera family. Actually," I said, "I don't personally know of anyone who has had a murder in their family."

On the contrary, I really know many people who have a lot going for them. I believe we should stand up and declare that happy families are normal. If someone has misery, as Christians we will try to help them. But misery must not be understood as a normal way of life.

The Cocoon of Carefulness

Much as the cocoon protects the emerging butterfly until its time of entry into the world, so the Christian home provides the safe place for our children to develop without harmful interference. If one would try to *help* the butterfly by opening the cocoon, the results would be disastrous. What could have become a graceful creation in its full development would be a stunted, weak creature. Premature exposure has marred its beauty and robbed it of a future.

The only way to insure our children's tomorrow is to cradle their growth today in the cocoon of our love and carefulness concerning everything that touches their lives. They should be afforded the opportunity of that marvelous experience called childhood. And it should last until they are ready to emerge into the adult environment. As parents, we need to be aware of the environment that touches our children's lives at all times. We cannot assume that the world is a safe place for our children today because it was safe for us as children.

It's a Different World

My sister and I were getting ready for bed one Friday evening when we heard footsteps on the porch. "Who could that be at this hour?" we wondered. Mom and Dad had left us to care for ourselves overnight while they took a short fishing trip. "Who is it?" we called tentatively through the door.

It was Mom and Dad. What were they doing? They must have forgotten something, we thought. I shall never forget the extreme happiness and security I felt as my father said with a little laugh, "We got lonely for you girls and decided to come back and get you. Grab your things. You're going with us."

Privately my mother said to me, "I told your daddy, 'If you'd be happier with them here, let's just go back and get them.'" I felt fortunate to have parents who wanted to share their lives with us.

Do we fully appreciate what this kind of loving atmosphere means to children? Parents are almost as God to children, especially in their early years. An atmosphere of caring and acceptance means everything to young children. My sister and I enjoyed that kind of caring atmosphere in our home.

However, the story I just related happened more than 30 years ago. That was before the prevalence of family breakdown. When I was a girl, rock music lyrics did not suggest that children rebel against parents, or that we should consider suicide. When we were growing up it was really out of the question for anyone to get drunk or try drugs. I can only remember one teenage girl in our school who became pregnant before marriage. We didn't worry about whether homosexuality should be accepted as an alternate life style. Most of us weren't exactly sure what it meant to be homosexual, anyway.

Today some surveys conclude that more than 50 percent of teens between 15 and 19 years old are sexually active. One in 10 teenagers becomes pregnant each year—twice the number since 1973. According to Josh McDowell, 500,000 children will attempt suicide this year. More than a million kids will run away from home.[1]

School Daze

It is difficult for parents to realize that there has been such a drastic change in the social environment since they were in high school. As an example, let's make a comparison of what were defined as "offenses" in high schools in 1940 and in 1980. The top offenses in public schools in 1940 were running in hallways, chewing gum, wearing improper clothing (including leaving shirt tail out), making noise, and not putting paper in wastebaskets. In 1980 the top offenses were robbery, assault, personal theft, burglary, drug abuse, arson, bombing, alcohol abuse, carrying weapons, absenteeism, vandalism, murder and extortion. Twelve of the offenses listed for 1980 are felonies.[2]

The Disappearing Family

In 1960, society defined a family as a husband and wife with or without children. The consensus was that religion was a positive influence on American family life and should be encouraged. Prayer was not only legal, but also common, as an opening exercise in the public school classroom. Now there is not even agreement by authorities on what constitutes a family. Broken homes, homosexual couples, or any combination of adults and children, married or otherwise, constitute family diversity in the minds of many.

More than 16 million U.S. children live with only one parent. If present trends continue, 61 percent of all children will spend some time in a single-parent household before they are 18! Five hundred thousand children across the U.S.A. are in foster care, perhaps five million in and out of the system annually (*USA Today*, 1993).

Even the place of children in the family is being disputed in our courts. A recent Illinois court ruling concerning the relationship of parents to children stated, "To hold that a child is the property of his parents is to deny the humanity of the child. [The child] belongs to no one but himself" (*USA Today*, 1993).

Added to these disappointing facts are the growing problems of alcohol and drug abuse, violence, and mental illness in American homes. During any one-year period, an estimated 41 million adults suffer some form of mental disorder—52 million if substance abuse is included (*USA Today*, August 14, 1993). All of these situations contribute to the deteriorating state of families in our nation.

A Decadent Society

It has been proven throughout history that a nation is no stronger than its moral fiber. Following the unraveling of the former Soviet Union and the demise of the communist system, the leaders of those countries began to openly acknowledge their need for spiritual input. They saw that there was no other way to rebuild a disillusioned, devastated people than to open the way for spiritual renewal. Amazingly, what the former communist nations are asking Americans to help them learn is what we have ceased to understand as a nation.

We have abandoned the moral education of our children in the public schools and have made a mockery of it in the media. Again, the results of this irresponsible approach to education can be seen in figures compiled by William Bennett, U.S. Secretary of Education. His statistics show that during the past 30 years violent crime has risen 560 percent, illegitimate births have increased 400 percent, divorce rates have quadrupled, teenage suicide has risen 200 percent and student S.A.T. scores have dropped 80 points.[3]

This same analysis shows that juvenile crime has quadrupled, the number of children living in single-parent homes has tripled, and the time spent by the average American watching television has doubled to nearly 50 hours per week. Bennett's comment on his depressing findings was, "It's almost as if we have been conducting an unwitting social experiment, saying, 'Let's have children. Let's not raise them. Let's not teach them right values. Let's support them entirely on government, and let's see how they turn out.' Now the results are in."

The Spirit of the Age

Is this a sign of the times? Is society, as we have known it, simply evolving downward into decadence? More accurately, we could say it's the spirit of the age. There is a powerful force motivating the trends of our society. We have not simply lost our appreciation for what we have as a nation, nor have we outgrown the commitment to the traditional American family, as some would suggest. The problem is rather that various groups and organizations have orchestrated the undermining of the American family. There has been a determined design, especially in our educational systems, to legislate against the value system of our fathers that was based on biblical principles.

One movement has written "The New Age Blueprint" to help formulate their goals for our children. One of their tenants is that "patriotism to one's country must be abolished and all national barriers destroyed to build a new one world order." Another tenant relating to family states, "The traditional family unit is not desirable for Aquarian, or New Age. The children belong to the government, to the world, and to the community...not to their parents."[5]

What were we thinking in the 1960's when "The Age of Aquarius" was just a pop song? No one told us that "Puff The Magic Dragon" was a song about marijuana, or that "Lucy in the Sky With Diamonds" was a code song referring to LSD (the first letters in the main words of the song). In these subtle ways we were introduced to the spirit of the age and were prepared to receive the philosophy called the New Age that denies God and most of our traditional values.

Swimming Upstream

With this negative backdrop of problems in today's society, it should not be surprising that rearing children today is fraught with difficulties. Once parents realize that we are living in a different world from the one in which we grew up, they will know where the battle lines are drawn. Pity the parent who takes the ostrich approach, as if hiding will somehow make this world go away.

The important thing to realize is that the world system is hostile to the Christian purpose—more hostile than it has ever been! Parents who have a commitment to win their children for the Kingdom must make up their minds that they will be constantly swimming upstream against a decadent society that has no sympathy with their ideals. They must seek their strength in God and in the community of the Church to save their children from the evil and prepare them for useful lives in the Kingdom of God.

Notes

1. Zig Ziglar, *Raising Positive Kids in a Negative World*, (Nashville, Tennessee: Thomas Nelson Pub., 1985), p. 36.
2. Ibid., p. 25.
3. William J. Bennett, "The Index of Leading Cultural Indicators," (Published in Kingsport-Times News, 9/3/93).
4. Ibid.
5. Texe Marrs, *Ravaged By the New Age*, (Austin, Texas: Living Truth Pub., 1989), pp. 19-23.

Chapter 7

As a Man Thinketh

In very simple terms, as William Bennett's analysis showed, when moral education has decreased, social ills have soared. I like Bennett's definition of the purpose of education: "to engage in the architecture of souls." This definition emphasizes the development of moral character. Obviously the priority of public education today has been placed on individualism, self–realization, and personal choice rather than on moral character. This humanistic philosophy has shaped the thinking of our country. It is firmly entrenched in the educational system, government agencies and the media. It is the accepted way to think in a society that has, by and large, turned its back on the Christian ethic.

The truth of the Bible has been rejected because it requires a belief in teachings that are absolute in nature. Certain virtues, normative patterns, and laws for human behavior are always true. They will never change. Accepting the fact of "absolutes" is the opposite of the relative thinking of the humanist. The humanist believes that A is A, but that A can sometimes be B. He believes that situations effect what is true. Above all else he believes that man must be free to make his own choices: not based on any set of principles or laws, but based on what he thinks.

As a way of thinking, humanism causes men to build societies based upon personal rights and self-realization, a philosophy of selfishness. As the Russian writer, Dostoevski, said in *The Brothers Karamazov*, "If there is no God, then everything is permitted!"[1] If we accept that philosophy, then, of course debauchery and crime are inevitable.

If It Feels Good

Permissiveness is the term that best describes the mentality of the humanistic thinker. Because there is no absolute value system in the religion of humanism, promiscuity is not related to the truth of God's Word, but to what my choices are and how it will best benefit me. As a result of our schools teaching that philosophy, 72 percent of all high school seniors have had sexual intercourse. Nearly one-fifth (19 percent) have had at least four partners. Three million teens have sexually transmitted diseases, and AIDS is the sixth leading cause of death among young people ages 15 through 24 (*USA Today*, January 12, 1994).

We have reaped the harvest from the humanistic seeds that have been carefully sown by those committed to a philosophy that is the basis of immoral systems throughout the world. And the spoiling "through philosophy and empty deception" referred to in the Scriptures has been our portion (see Col. 2:8 NAS).

In my personal experience with children and teenagers, I have found that they want to be taught the right way to think. They are actually very insecure concerning their ability to function in life, and they welcome loving instruction in this area. It is the adult humanists, not the teenagers, that demand such unreasonable rights. Teenagers can be just as easily influenced by biblical thought as by liberal philosophies. They are looking for answers. We need to care enough to teach them the way to successful living.

A sample of the humanistic ideas foisted upon students in New York City comes from the Center for Disease Control, a federal agency, and is entitled "A Teenager's Bill of Rights":

(1) I have the right to think for myself.

(2) I have the right to decide whether to have sex and whom to have it with.

(3) I have the right to use protection when I have sex.

(4) I have the right to buy and use condoms.

(5) I have the right to express myself.

(6) I have the right to ask for help if I need it.

And they will need it! When I read this to our congregation in a Sunday service, our teenagers laughed and ridiculed the unreasonableness of the proposition. They have been taught well enough to see the other end of such an irresponsible life style.

Who Is Designing Your Thoughts?

Though the great emphasis of humanists is upon choice and what you think, there is no such thing as bias-free curriculum or objective news-reporting. When the New York City school system offers first-grade curriculum that pictures two lesbians or two homosexual parents in a positive light, that is not bias-free. Or when they want to tell young children that "gay is just one more kind of love," they are not bias-free. They are endorsing the homosexual life style that the Bible condemns.

Whether it is the school curriculum or the nightly news report, everything has a message. Every movie or book has its own message. The person presenting it is communicating his philosophy. Every TV program has a message, even the commercials, and it can often be very subtle. These influencers are the powers that have molded the thinking of an entire society. That is why protection of our children from wrong exposure is so important. Once an impression is made, it is difficult to change.

This concept, as the Moravians taught it to the parents of future missionaries, was: "Protect them from evil influence and harmful impressions." That requires diligent vigilance over our children's lives. We must realize that whoever is talking to our kids is the one who is influencing them.

You can count on Hollywood to teach them to "just say yes." The school curriculum, the media, and their peers will bombard them with a philosophy that is the opposite of Christian principles. A recent survey for the book, *The Media Elite,* found that most leading television journalists and news anchors label themselves politically as liberal. Ninety percent are pro-choice, seventy-five percent believe homosexuality is morally acceptable, and only eight percent attend religious services regularly. These percentages are very similar for Hollywood writers and producers. Through TV and movies, these people are teaching your children their personal values.[2]

As Charles Colson has said, "If you thought movies were just entertainment, think again. Every movie producer has a worldview and a personal philosophy that he expresses through the film."[3]

What's Wrong with Rights?

I believe that an understanding of humanism, the present philosophy of our culture, is absolutely necessary if we want to preserve our youth from spiritual, mental, and moral decay. For this reason I prepared a complete study of the history and philosophy of humanism for our church. We needed to have our minds cleansed of this philosophy of the world and to think God's thoughts after Him.[4]

God's Word teaches that a child left to himself will give shame to his mother, and that if you correct your son he shall give you rest, and give delight to your soul (see Prov. 29:15,17). The Bible also lays the responsibility squarely on the parents to "train up a child in the way he should go," not according to the choices he presents to you (see Prov. 22:6). Of course there are no biblical rights for abortion, premarital sex, or birth control for unmarried teens. Abortion is called "murder" and premarital sex is called "fornication" in the Bible.

The real problem with "rights" or "choices," as we saw earlier, goes back to Adam and Eve in the garden of Eden. God gave them many legitimate things from which to choose, but He commanded them to stay away from the tree of knowledge of good and evil (Gen. 2:16-17). Unfortunately, the serpent deceived them to believe that if they ate of the forbidden tree they would become as gods. The subtle suggestion was that God was not serving their best interests by protecting them from harm through His commandment, but that He was depriving them of good things (see Gen. 3:4-5).

The right to choose independently of God's command became more important to Adam and Eve than their fellowship with God and their obedience to Him. But God has created man to be limited to the laws He has set for man's growth and blessing. Obedience to God's Word is a wonderful protection that preserves us from the intended ravages of the enemy upon our lives. We can trust God that His Word and His way for us will keep us in a place of blessing, though it may require the sacrifice of immediate gratification (as with teenagers and their sexual desires).

The right of choice does not produce the freedom it promises despite all the clamoring for it. Choices based upon the wrong value system enslave mankind to his own lusts and deprive him of true creativity. For example, the Children's Defense Fund defends the legal rights of children against parents and government. It wants to give children the right to choose whether to attend school, get a job, or have an abortion. It puts the authority of the state right in your home and allows them to take your child and give it to state professionals. It gives children the right to privacy (from parents) and the right to divorce their parents.[5]

Such legislation denies the developmental stages in childhood and adolescence that warrant adult protection. The humanists who have devised these ordinances want a world with neither parental authority nor childhood innocence. That is not freedom. It enslaves the child to a pseudo-maturity he is not ready for and burdens him with the crushing load of decisions beyond his ability or concern.

A Discipline of Fools

The Book of Proverbs teaches that the man who yields to the adulterous woman submits to the discipline of a fool (see Prov. 7:22 ASV). Adultery becomes a discipline, but the result is to train the man to be a fool. Humanism has been a discipline of the mind to those who receive it, but its fruit is only palatable to fools. The statistics I have quoted show the futility of the philosophy of humanism, and sadly, the destruction that results from the implementation of foolish choices. To clarify, let me state three great tenants of humanism:

(1) The purpose of man's life is the complete realization of his own personality.

(2) Man must seek his development now. Eternity is meaningless; even tomorrow is meaningless.

(3) The universe is self-existing. It was not created; it evolved. Therefore, man is his own god.[6]

Atheistic, secular humanism had its beginnings with the philosopher, Immanuel Kant, the first man to teach that if one thing is right, the exact opposite thing can also be right; it depends upon the thinker. This humanistic philosophy was later endorsed by Marx, Lenin, and Hegel, and became the basis for the communistic ideology. We have seen the fruit of that system.

Obviously, absolute thought based on the Scriptures teaches that if one thing is right, then its exact opposite must be wrong. Christian character cannot be developed when people adhere to a philosophy of relative choices. Humanistic thinking gives birth to such phrases as "Just this once won't matter," "If it feels good, do it," and "Boys will be boys." All of these ideas suggest living for self-gratification that militates against the development of godly character.

The public school teachers trained in humanism as well as the curricula they use teach the children to question everything and to make value judgments in areas that children are mentally and socially unprepared to consider—all in the name of freedom of thought. But the result is the undermining of the foundation of biblical values that deprives the student of the ability to think soundly.

Another Way to Think

According to the Bible, a sound mind is a gift of God to those who choose to obey His commands (see 2 Tim. 1:7). And the Scriptures teach that "As a man thinketh in his heart, so is he" (see Prov. 23:7). We must realize the extreme importance of directing our children's minds to the values that will guarantee their success in life. The value that humanists have placed on educating a generation according to their godless philosophy underscores, in a negative way, the importance of how we think. Humanism results in the self-destruction of all those who embrace its philosophy. True success can only be realized through the development of godly character. Godly character is developed by receiving the truth of the Word of God and thinking according to its principles.

The Scriptures show us the remedy for the wrong kind of thinking. They tell us that we should have our minds renewed through God's Word (see Rom. 12:2). Our natural, unrenewed minds have formed patterns of thought that are hostile toward God. Only the Holy Spirit, working in us through the power of the Word of God, can deliver us from what the Bible calls a "carnal" mind. And to be carnally minded is death, but to be spiritually minded is life and peace (see Rom. 8:6-7).

In the previous chapter, I quoted some frightening statistics relating to mental illness and mental disorder because of substance abuse. These are representative of the lack of peace in the minds of millions of Americans. Added to these extreme cases, we have the unsound thinking fostered by the philosophy of humanism that pervades most of the public educational, social, and judicial systems of America, not to mention the alliance of most of the media spokesmen and performers. We have seen the fruit of this thinking in the rampant promiscuity, violence, and the general state of social misery of our nation.

To prepare a generation to think God's thoughts after Him so that they can know His purposes, we must be delivered from an unsound mind ourselves and instruct our children that there is another way to think.

Notes

1. Charles Colson, *A Dance With Deception*, (Dallas, Texas: Word Publishing, 1993), p. 202.

2. Ibid., pp. 18, 81-104.
3. Ibid.
4. A copy of this humanism course including eight cassette tapes and course syllabus is available for a cost of $35.00 by writing to:

   Shekinah Ministries
   394 Glory Road
   Blountville, Tennessee 37617

5. Charles Colson. *A Dance With Deception*, (Dallas, Texas: Word Publishing, 1993), p. 169.
6. Paul Kurtz, ed., *Humanist Manifestos, I and II*, (Buffalo, New York: Prometheus Books, 1973), pp. 8-9.

Chapter 8

Peace in My Day

The disciplining of children is a discipline for parents. It is a process that demands diligence. Parents must have a determination that they will accept the responsibility for molding their children for God's purpose.

One of the most amazing biblical examples of a delinquent parent is King Hezekiah. His selfish, irresponsible attitude was revealed in his response to the prophet Isaiah's warning regarding the potential end of his children:

> *Then said Isaiah to Hezekiah, Hear the word of the Lord of hosts: Behold, the days come, that all this is in thine house, and that which thy fathers have laid up in store until this day, shall be carried to Babylon: nothing shall be*

> *left, saith the Lord. And of thy sons that shall issue from thee, which thou shalt beget, shall they take away; and they shall be eunuchs in the palace of the king of Babylon.*
>
> Isaiah 39:5-7

Hezekiah's unbelievable response to such a predicted judgment follows:

> *...Good is the word of the Lord which thou hast spoken. He said moreover, For there shall be peace and truth in my days!*
>
> Isaiah 39:8

Who can believe that a father would be willing to accept such a negative prophecy regarding his children and call it good? But his motive is seen in his statement, "There shall be peace in my days." The mentality of "peace in my day" is the prevailing attitude of the undisciplined parent who rears undisciplined children. When parents put their own comfort and convenience above the responsibility of rearing godly children, they are embracing that mentality. Of course they would like to see their children turn out right, but there is a price to be paid for anything that is truly of value.

People are willing to pay whatever it costs for things on which they place a high value. Can anything be of greater value than children who love and serve the Lord with all their hearts? We must be willing to pay the price of properly disciplining our children to make this happen.

How to "Shoot" Your Kids

> *Lo, children are an heritage of the Lord: and the fruit of the womb is his reward. As arrows are in the hand of a mighty man; so are children of the youth.*
>
> Psalm 127:3-4

The psalmist described children as arrows in the hand of a mighty man, a warrior. To continue this analogy to its end, we could say that it is not until these arrows are directed and shot by a "mighty" parent, one who is spiritually disciplined, that they will hit the mark of God's purpose. Parents have a real need to learn how to "shoot" their kids into the purposes of God.

An arrow cannot shoot itself. It is a weapon waiting to be launched. Prevailing philosophy suggests that somehow the direction for that arrow is found inside itself. But how opposed this is to God's plan for the counsel and training of our children. A "peace in my day" mentality is prevalent because society as a whole has embraced the humanistic idea that children's lives should not be guided; and that since they are basically good they will make the right choices if left to themselves. Of course, sad experience has proved that this is not true. Children must be taught how to make right choices that are based in biblical values.

Because this humanistic philosophy has infiltrated the thinking of our children, it often requires confrontation with them to come against their selfish choices or worldly preferences. It is more peaceful not to "fight the system" by resisting the children's wrong thinking. But if we settle for this kind of peace, as parents we are being irresponsible to the command of God to train our children in His ways (see Deut. 6:6-9). At the root of this shirking of duty is hypocrisy. Some parents pretend to be blind to what their children are doing or saying in order to avoid confrontation. They convince themselves that if they just "leave it alone," things will work out.

These parents may give lip service to their responsibility, yet as they live out their lives they never take proper action. We need only to remember God's commendation of Abraham to see that God is pleased with the parent who will put what he believes into action. God knew that Abraham would command his household in the ways of God.

Looking more closely at the proverb, "Train up a child in the way he should go: and when he is old, he will not depart from it" (Prov. 22:6), we see that this powerful promise is conditioned upon the process of *training*. The promise is not given for teaching or praying, but for training. In the training process, those arrows are aimed every day. The responsible parent is unwilling to turn them over to the schools or to the state. They are his arrows; he must train them. He is responsible to shoot them straight into the purposes of God.

The Power of Training

The following maxim expresses the reward for careful training:

> Sow an act and you reap a **habit**.
> Sow a habit and you reap a **character**.
> Sow a character and you reap a **destiny**.

Without proper parental direction and discipline, a child is aimless. He has no goals, so he never knows when he is succeeding. Because of his need for direction, he will begin to take upon himself the identity or goals of others he admires, such as a sports hero or Hollywood performer. The goals of these heroes are both impossible to attain for most children and useless for the Joshua Generation young person. The child thus left to himself, though he is not aimless, becomes misdirected into futile pursuits.

Without proper goals and a plan to achieve them, the unguided child begins to focus on the immediate because his mental powers are not developed fully enough to give him foresight and discipline on his own. This immature focus leads to irresponsible self-gratification in many forms that is destructive to young minds and bodies. Responsible parents who understand the importance of giving direction to their children are those who have discovered the biblical principle of the power of training.

Training vs. Teaching

Training is a discipline that begins where teaching ends. Some parents think they have trained their children when they have only taught them principles. Five-year-old Paul caused his mother to grapple with this reality one day when she brought him to our church sanctuary. We have taught our parents to bring their children with them to the thirty minutes we dedicate to pre-service prayer before each of our church services begins. Paul was unusually restless during the prayer time that day, first making little noises, then tearing paper. Finally his mother pleaded with him, "You know this is prayer time. Stop doing that and pray." Little Paul answered quietly, "I don't know how to pray." He had been taught what prayer time was, but not trained to pray. His mother then had him kneel beside her as she began to pray with him, using a vocabulary he could understand and including him in her time of prayer. That is training.

The following comparison between teaching and training may be helpful for parents to understand what is involved in each:

Teaching	*Training*
Causes another to know (Mind-directed)	Causes another to do (Will-directed)
Gives knowledge	Gives skill
Fills the mind	Shapes the habits
Brings to the child what he did not have before	Enables a child to make use of what he has

This definition of training may help some parents to understand that they are only teaching their children when they think they are training them. They are giving them the right information, but are not providing the framework in which the information can become a part of the child's life through proper discipline. Andrew Murray's definition of training is "accustoming the child to do easily and willingly what is commanded. Doing right, doing it habitually, doing it from his choice—this is what we aim at."[1] As long as there is a fight, a continual dealing with resistance, we may be in the process of training our children, but we must recognize that they are not yet trained if they are still expressing disagreement.

Our children join our worship service, which they enjoy very much because they are trained to be a part of it. They lift their hands, bow, dance, and sing. They do everything we do. We want them to be exposed to this level of worship and we want them to follow the same biblical patterns we adults do to express love to Jesus.

After worship on Sunday mornings, our children are dismissed to their own nurseries and special classes through grade five. The older children and youth remain in the sanctuary for the morning sermon. They are taught to take notes on the sermons along with the adults and to enter in to all that is happening. Though we recognize the special needs of different age groups, we have not segregated them so that they feel their worship and church involvement is completely different from ours.

Will-Training vs. Will-Breaking

As we have seen, the end of training is teaching a child how to make his own right choices. It is neither leaving all the choices to him, nor is it demanding obedience without understanding. Unfortunately, some parents have thought that the way to train a child is to break his will, that is, to bring the pressure of an external force directly upon that will and cause the will to give way under the pressure of that force. Coercing a will does not result in a trained will, for the child will only conform as long as your restraint or his fear of you prevails.

The proper way to *train* a child's will is to lovingly influence the child so that he is ready to choose or decide for himself in favor of the right course of action. All the way through a child's training, he ought to feel your approval for his right choices, and know the legitimate consequences of his wrong choices. The right place for punishment in a child's training is as a penalty attached to a wrong choice, not as force applied to compel a certain action against his choice.

Purpose as the Motivator

In our church community, we are continually holding before our children their biblical purpose in life: to bring glory to God and to fulfill His will for their lives. It is wonderful for children and young people to see a demonstration in the local church that shows them what they can have for their lives if they choose to follow God. Throughout their lives they have watched as God's Spirit has moved in our meetings, causing people to love and support one another.

They have heard the prophetic word and the song of the Lord on a regular basis as it blesses the congregation. They have both written praise songs themselves and sung those that others in the church have written. Our children have learned to pray anointed prayers for burdens the Lord has given them. They have experienced revival and moves of repentance, so they know what it is to have visitations of the Lord. And they like it. They understand that this is the purpose for which they were born. Their hearts are being filled with the purpose of God, what He has promised to do in the earth, and they are establishing their personal goals so they can be a part of it.

They have been taught how God has used children and teenagers throughout history, and they know they have a destiny that is just as exciting. They are constantly aware of God's purpose for life, and are pursuing their personal goals to fulfill it. They have traveled to mission fields and have had their minds and hearts thrilled with the harvest. It is too late to entice them with the plodding predictableness of the mundane they see in the world. Neither are they interested in the self-destructive pleasures it offers.

So when a parent is training the will of a child, he is holding up to that child the purpose for his life, asking him how he is going to set particular goals in light of that purpose. For example, in our church, a young person can choose to be in the Festival Singers evangelistic outreach team involved in mime, dance and song; or he can choose to be involved in activities outside the church that may not be sinful in themselves, but would take him away from his purpose. Our parents understand that the church's outreach activities help to develop a capacity in our young people for the work of God and the fulfillment of their destiny. So they encourage them to make the choices that will promote the fulfillment of their purpose. (Of course there are some activities that are not up for discussion. Children are expected to come to church services, prayer meetings, and other church functions as a part of their family that forms the Body of Christ.)

Meaning of Life

There must be a true commitment to what we say we believe on the part of both the child and the parent if life is to be lived with real purpose. Unfortunately some parents use the right language, but the commitment is not in their hearts. Other things in life have more meaning to them and this is communicated to the children by the way they live their lives.

A few years ago I did some teaching on the *meaning of life*. It seemed to have an impact on the congregation and some parents had been discussing it in the presence of their children. One of the parents was having a difficult time with her three-year-old son, Tim, on a particular day. Finally, in exasperation she sighed, "Tim, what is mother going to do with you?" "I don't know, Mommy," Tim replied. "I think maybe I just don't know the meaning of life." Such an admission from a three-year-old may seem amusing to us, but he was beginning to grasp a concept that he needed help to make choices and to learn how to live. Our children will surprise us with their capacity for understanding spiritual things if we continually expose them to anointed teaching and to the moving of the Spirit of God.

Parents who commit themselves to the godly task of training their children will know the joy that God intended for children to bring to them. They must first be committed to the goal of bringing glory to God themselves, before they can expect to have children who will follow their example. Then they can depend on the Holy Spirit to give wisdom and help them to lovingly influence their children to be motivated by the eternal purpose for which God created them.

Notes

1. Andrew Murry, *How To Raise Your Children For Christ,* (Minneapolis, Minnesota, Bethany House Pub., 1975), p. 124.

Chapter 9

The Kingdom Is Exciting!

"It's almost too good to be true! It's more than we ever expected! Tell the parents that their teenagers are not homesick. I hope I can get them to come home!"

The call came from Mexico. The excited youth worker's words tumbled out. "The youth did their mime called 'Wounded Soldier' and the Mexican people came streaming forward asking for ministry. There was such a move of the Spirit that the youth minister never could preach his sermon. Can you believe it? The kids are going nuts!" (This is a positive assessment.)

We have heard so much about the attractiveness of the world that we almost develop an expectation, it seems, of losing our young people to worldly pursuits. Once the exciting possibilities of life in the Spirit have been presented to young people, why would they choose the ordinary things that any person in the world can have? When they are clearly taught concerning the ravages of the world, they can respond excitedly to opportunities to minister the gospel. The problem is that we Christians have not always made the good things of the Kingdom attractive and exciting.

The world, on the contrary, has done an excellent job of making the most boring situations seem interesting. For example, the advertising world tries to mold values by making their products sound exciting. Really now, a certain toothpaste doesn't cause you to be more at ease and charming when you're with the opposite sex. Even a red sports car doesn't make people really like you. Those ideas are all a matter of advertising imagery—creating an illusion that makes people believe a particular product is the most exciting.

Privilege or Duty?

What attitude do we project to our children about going to church? Is it perceived as a privilege or an obligation? Children pick up on that. I have taught that we "get" to go to church, or we "get" to go to prayer meetings. Our children feel positive about their church involvements, as eight-year-old Joshua proved when he told his friend, "Sunday and Wednesday nights we have church. Saturday night we have prayer meetings. Tuesday night is orchestra practice. The rest of the nights are 'nothing nights.'" Why? Because the functions of the ministry were the "something" nights in his life. Christian parents can build that positive perspective of involvement in the Kingdom of God into their children.

Proper Involvements

It is not true that children are excitement mongers that cannot be satisfied unless they are being entertained or are involved in some whirl of activity every moment. Our experience has been that children can enjoy the presence of God, sitting quietly in a prayer meeting or joining in a worship service. They are satisfied to be a part of their parents' lives and activities when they are properly affirmed and accepted.

We readily admit that children like activity; they like challenges and they like variety. The answer to that need is to provide activities and worthwhile endeavors for your children that promote God's purposes and do not undermine what you have been building in your child. Questionable amusements don't even need to be considered. The world system is often incompatible with a life style that encourages godliness.

Children love camping, hiking, boating, and skiing. Did you ever see a "rebel" leading a horse? Taking walks and reading are also satisfying and wholesome activities for children. Children, whose activities are of a more natural involvement, are less given to the rebellion that is promoted through much of secular entertainment, video games, and all that the media offers. Avoiding the "spectator" mentality that is developed, even by watching acceptable videos, is important if we are to develop our children's desires to be involved in meaningful activity.

What children really want is their parents' time and attention. They want to be a part of your life. They would be just as happy fishing with Dad as they would be listening to rock music. When you go to visit someone in the hospital, there is no reason one of your children can't go along. Seeing you pray for the sick will teach them how to show the love of Jesus in those situations.

I know a ministry family whose three children followed in their parents' footsteps, becoming ministers themselves. One of those children tells about how he used to sit with his mother when she would pray. His mother was an outstanding minister who influenced many others to serve God in her lifetime. He recounted his experience when his mother would say, "Let's go pray." Then after she prayed she would say to him, "God just spoke to me." She would get up and go tell people what God had said to her. He continued, "As a child, what I never could figure out is that I was sitting right there beside her, and I never heard anything." He may never have heard anything, but by listening to his mother pray time after time, he learned how to pray himself and get an answer from God. Now that is exciting! His mother let him know that they were on exciting business. They learned as children how to build an effective ministry through God.

Christianity is not philosophy, nor is it a theory. If it is anything at all, it is a *way of life*. If we do not live what we believe, we have missed the point. Jesus came to give us a life to be lived abundantly (see Jn. 10:10). The perspective that we as parents present to our children will form the outlook they have on life. If we serve God out of obligation, that will be our children's approach. If they see that we have dedicated our lives to a loving Savior who allows us to serve Him and blesses us in return, they will feel privileged to be a part of that life style. Take your children with you on your spiritual journey. Make them a part of your life and worship. Let them know that you expect them to follow in your footsteps as you follow Jesus.

Eternity in Their Hearts

Dispelling Foolishness

The Scriptures teach that foolishness is bound in the heart of a child (see Prov. 22:15). This is a fact.

The word foolishness, also translated "silliness" or "folly," is derived from the same Hebrew root meaning "perverse." The reason this verse in Proverbs tells us to "drive foolishness far from the child" is because it is a perversion of what God intends for children, which is joy and gladness.

Foolishness is driven out of the heart of the child through discipline and training. Then, filling the heart with a God-given vision for life helps to displace the foolishness that has been bound up there. Those who serve God are the happiest people on earth. But we must understand that true happiness is beyond the idea of having fun. If we have fun at times, that is fine. If we don't, it doesn't matter because that isn't our pursuit. Fulfilling the purpose of God in the earth is our goal in life. Though that may sometimes lead us through difficulties, God has promised to give us joy that no man can take away from us (see Jn. 16:22).

No amusement in the world can come close to making such a promise. The Kingdom life in the realm of supernatural experience and relationship with the Lord of the universe is the true source of joy. God is in favor of laughing. He laughs Himself (see Ps. 2:4). He rejoices over us (see Zeph. 3:17). He gives us joy unspeakable and full of glory (see 1 Pet. 1:8). His Word tells us that we are to rejoice all the time in Him (see Phil. 4:4). This joy has nothing to do with silliness or foolishness that are perversions of the true joy of the Spirit that comes only from relationship with Jesus. Our amusement-oriented, fun-seeking society would not understand that there is something much more exciting and consistently satisfying than can be offered by Disney World. Only those who find their purpose in God will realize these promises of God in their lives.

When God's eternal purpose to have a family in the earth that is like Him begins to fill our hearts, then we see our ministries as a part of that wonder. As we view the nations of the earth, we begin to function with eternity in our hearts. We begin to be filled with desire, as the Moravians used to say, "to win for the Lamb the reward of His suffering." Experiencing such divine love will become our driving motivation to make it possible for our children and others to be a part of God's eternal purpose.

Youth Missions

Our teenagers worked with me in the great harvest in Ukraine during a summer evangelistic crusade. As they gave their testimonies and did their mimes and dances, they saw hundreds of lives transformed before their eyes. They thrilled to see 400 Ukranian military students stand to receive Jesus Christ! As they moved among them giving out New Testaments, they were both broken and excited to witness the hunger for God in a people prohibited from hearing His Word for seventy years. They felt they were a part of fulfilling the prophecy, "The people who sat in darkness have seen a great light" (see Mt. 4:16).

What a privilege to bring the light of God to a people who do not know Him! Can the transformation of a life compare to a Nintendo game? Can the winning of a former Communist Party boss to Jesus Christ compare to high school parties? Playing church is not exciting. But having a sense of reliving the Book of Acts, experiencing the opening of nations, and the establishing of the gospel in other lands is!

Recently I taught our church the principle of immediacy as it relates to the harvest. Jesus said that when the harvest is ripe, the harvester puts in the sickle immediately (see Mk. 4:29). This is the only time to reap the harvest. One of our teenagers who has felt a call to missions was so inspired that she posed this question to our youth pastor: "If high school students can take their own tutor with them so that they can play tennis professionally, why couldn't I take a tutor and go to Ukraine to work in the mission field?" She really understands the urgency of a ripe harvest and wants to be a part of it.

Realizing Spiritual Goals

It wasn't that our youth were having a good experience visiting a foreign country; it was that they were touching the spiritual realm where dreams come true. It was a place where they stepped out in faith with just what they had and gave it all from their hearts, and they began to see the miracles of God. They were not waiting for *someday*. They are the Church of today.

They are now planning their trip to Ukraine again for the summer, getting their own funds by selling doughnuts or doing whatever they can. It is not easy. It is hard work and requires discipline. It stretches them in the realms of both faith and ability. They pray, they learn a whole musical program of mime, dance, and song, besides earning their money to go. And once they arrive at their missions destination they go through another set of difficulties: stagefright, culture shock, and Big Mac attacks. But they end up with joy that no one can take away from them!

Our children and teenagers worked in our Kid's Fest locally as well, in which we brought in housing project kids to be taught about Jesus, fed, and entertained for a week. They minister at nursing homes on a regular basis and work in child evangelism with puppets. They know how to give their testimonies and how to pray for other children who want to give their hearts to Jesus. They also help in the church nurseries and work with our *Kingdom Kids'* training program. They are involved in a group called Festival Singers, which gives them an opportunity to minister evangelistically in several community festivals where other secular singing and talent groups perform. They simply go to let their musical program be their testimony about the good things God is doing.

So much of what the world has to offer is merely a spectator game, listening or watching. The Kingdom is exciting because it involves actually doing the thing that is happening and becoming a part of what God is doing. It provides many challenges and learning experiences. The sky is the limit because the Holy Spirit is working with them and through them.

Work of the Holy Spirit

We can expect the unusual and the unpredictable as we accept the reality that the same Holy Spirit who wrote the Book of Acts is the one who is directing the work of the Church today. We can trust the Holy Spirit to be the same life force in us and in our children that He was in the Book of Acts. He directs and empowers the person whose life is fully given over to the will of God. As He walked in fellowship with the disciples, He will do the same for us and our children. This reality of power, direction, and supernatural experience is what makes the Kingdom exciting. You will never find anything like it short of Heaven!

Chapter 10

What If It Doesn't Work?

Many parents today live in dread of losing their children, either spiritually or physically, to the world system. The changes in society's values the last thirty years have been bewildering, and the destructive elements to children's lives, staggering. Admittedly, without supernatural intervention, it is a frightening prospect to attempt to rear children who will follow God in this ungodly world.

God does not want us to be anxious about our children. Our assurance as Christian parents that our children will serve God is grounded in the promises of God's Word. He gave our children to us, and He gave us His Word as a blueprint for producing a godly seed. We do have the supernatural intervention we need to rear godly children.

Though parents are responsible to train their children in the ways of God, our children are not preserved merely by our doing everything right as far as we are able. In His love, God has given us the Holy Spirit, the power of prayer, and His covenant promises of His supernatural intervention in our lives.

A Covenant-Keeping God

> *And I will establish My covenant between Me and thee and thy seed after thee in their generations for an everlasting covenant, to be a God unto thee, and to thy seed after thee.*
>
> Genesis 17:7

God established His covenant with Abraham to be His God and the God of His seed. Every covenant that God institutes is sure. Fulfillment of His covenants is based on His faithfulness, not our perfection. And the promise of God to Abraham regarding his seed was not dependent upon Abraham's son Isaac. The recipient of a covenant is the parent. And the condition of walking in that covenant relationship with God is faith. As parents put their trust in the faithfulness of God's promises, they will see those promises fulfilled in their children's lives.

That is why Joshua could say with confidence, "...as for me *and my* house, we will serve the Lord" (Josh. 24:15 emphasis mine). And that is how Noah had confidence for his household in the face of impending worldwide destruction. God had said to Noah, "...Come thou and all thy house into the ark: for *thee* have I seen righteous before Me in this generation" (Gen. 7:1 emphasis mine). God's covenant was with Noah, a righteous man, but the blessing of God extended to his children as well.

Marking Our Children

As we have seen, God has given parents the responsibility for the proper training of their children. Throughout history from earliest times, God has shown His people how to separate their children unto His purposes. He gave Abraham the command to circumcise his sons as a sign of his covenant with God. A circumcised child was marked for God through the obedience of his parents. The New Testament teaches that our circumcision is of the heart by the work of the Holy Spirit. In obedience to God, we allow Him to cut away from us the sinfulness of our flesh and the ways of the world (see Rom. 2:29; Col. 2:11-14).

In that way we are marked for God's purposes in a covenant relationship with Him, and we can expect His promises to be fulfilled in our lives. As parents, we are responsible to preserve our children from the ways of the world, marking them for God's purposes. Then we can expect the Holy Spirit to do His work in their hearts as we prayerfully believe God to fulfill His covenant with us.

Job prayed for his children continually, offering sacrifices before God for them, in case they had sinned (see Job: 1:5). This biblical example of a godly parent teaches us that we cannot underestimate the importance of our spiritual responsibility in the preservation of our children. That is why it is so important that we learn to take time to seek God in prayer concerning our children.

As we sincerely give ourselves to the responsibility of marking our children for the Kingdom of God and preserving them from the world system, we can live in assurance that we are not working alone. There is no need to fear losing our children when we understand that our covenant-keeping God is working with us for their full salvation.

A Lamb for a House

God's covenant with Abraham was for the *preservation* of his seed, separating them from the world and making them a unique people. When God established His covenant with Moses and the people of Israel, He made provision for their *complete* salvation:

> *Speak ye unto all the congregation of Israel, saying, In the tenth day of this month they*

> *shall take to them every man a lamb, according to the house of their fathers,* ***a lamb for an house*** (emphasis mine).
>
> Exodus 12:3

Of course, this refers to the time in the history of God's people when the death angel was going to pass over Egypt and kill the first born of every house. The people of Israel, slaves in Egypt, could only escape this fate if they obeyed the command of God through Moses to slay a lamb, eat it, and sprinkle its blood on the doorposts of their homes. God promised them, "When I see the blood, I will pass over you" (Ex. 12:13). Through their obedience, the Passover lamb secured deliverance for the whole household.

We recognize this awesome event as the Old Testament picture of the slaying of our Passover Lamb, Jesus Christ. The entire household was gathered around that one Passover lamb, and all were spared the judgment of God because of their obedience to God's covenant. As parents partake of the life of Christ, centering their attentions on His provision for life, they will gather their children as well and bring them to the covenant provision of the blood of Christ.

Of course, every person in a home must be saved by personal faith in Christ, for there is no other way of salvation. But what the Old Testament reality of the Passover lamb teaches us, in type, is that the parents' faith in and obedience to the covenant promise of God brought protection from destruction and made the home a special place of God's awareness.

The Priesthood of Parents

Charles Usher, in his valuable little book, *The Prayer Life*, writes:

> Prayer alone can create a spiritual atmosphere in the home; for it opens the door for God to enter and also drive satan and all evil out. The heads of the home should take their right place, and rule in prayer; realizing that God has placed them there, and has made them responsible for its spiritual well-being.[1]

Parents are priests unto God for this two-fold purpose: (1) to present their children to God, and (2) to present God to their children.

Family Altar

One of the ways parents make their home a refuge is by emphasizing the importance of the family altar, a daily devotional time spent together as a family. The basic requirement for the family altar is to have an established time to gather together. Some parents have suggested that this is next to impossible because the family is involved in so many different activities.

Hard choices will need to be made to decide whether all these involvements are worthy of the price that will be paid for lack of prayer and family ministry to one another in the home. One of the reasons that our Christian homes have lost so many children to the world is that, in the childhood years, the wrong choices were made concerning the use of our children's time.

John Wesley's mother had a rule concerning recreation: "...never to spend more time in any matter of mere recreation in one day than she spent in private religious duties." In that way she made religious duties the priority of every day. We sometimes have the idea that if our involvements are not intrinsically wrong or sinful, it is alright to allow them. But the issue here is not a matter of right or wrong. It is a matter of not allowing other pursuits, however legitimate, to crowd out time for the family altar and spiritual fellowship in the home. Winning this battle is imperative to securing the safety of our children according to God's covenant promise.

If All Else Fails

There will be times when it seems that the parent has done what he knows to do, but it doesn't seem to be working. Children will occasionally have bouts of spiritual deadness or even antagonism toward the way they have been taught. The promises of God are still true. They just haven't yet been fulfilled for those children.

God has not promised that there will never be problems or inconsistencies in rearing our children. Children are just like adults; they have character lapses because their character is still being formed. They will make mistakes and disappoint us. They will sometimes be tempted, and at other times will become frustrated. Sometimes they will even feel like giving up. Haven't you?

I have known of a "model child" who one day begins to manifest problem attitudes. In these situations sometimes the parents become a greater problem than the child. They may unwittingly place more importance on what others think about their child's behavior (and ultimately, how it will reflect on the parent) than they place on the needs of the child. They panic simply because they have temporarily lost their grip on the promise of God. Problems don't need to shake our confidence in God's promises. It is in the difficult times that parents need to remember they have a covenant with a faithful God.

It is absolutely necessary for the parent to know, for his own sanity's sake, that God will come through. We walk by faith and not by sight, and childrearing is no exception to that faith walk. We have not yet seen all the things God will do to draw our errant child back to his rightful place. But it may take a little longer than we had anticipated. The child may be allowed to face some things in himself that neither we, as parents, nor he knew were there. This is a part of the process of God's dealing with His children. He has no grandchildren.

Prodigals

Jesus tells us the story of an errant son so that we can see the Father's heart in response to him (see Lk. 15:11-32). Isn't the father in this parable just like any other parent who made every provision and gave every spiritual advantage to his son? Yet there was still something in this prodigal son that had to be dealt with.

The father did not try to keep his son from leaving home. He even gave him provision for his sojourn. It is only a matter of time for a son who has lived in the blessing of the Lord to realize what he has lost by leaving home. Prodigals are the most unhappy sinners on earth because the incorruptible seed of God's Word in them refuses to die. The Holy Spirit is a nag every day of their lives; as the wonderful "hound of heaven," He will dog their heels.

Some prodigals get to the bottom more quickly than others, but they all eventually get their fill of sin. We have to trust God that the incorruptible seed of the Word in them will not be destroyed. After they have suffered the kind of abuse that the world can bring, they will begin to remember the blessings of the Father's house.

That is when they need to know that the door is open for them to return. The father in Jesus' parable received his prodigal back with tears and kisses, and restored him to his place as a son. He killed the fatted calf (not a skinny one of half-hearted forgiveness) and threw a party. His son had come back to life. And life was what mattered; not the prodigal's failures.

Certainly the prodigal choice is a hard way to learn. And for most Christian children, it will not be necessary to go that way. But for a few, there seems to be no other way. Just know, as a godly parent, that the fact that your child is even now in a far country does not change the promise of God. If you are suffering over a prodigal, pray for the incorruptible seed that is in him to rise up and fight the lies of the enemy that would try to destroy his life.

Great men of God have suffered this agony, and have also known the wonder of having their children restored. William Carey, the father of modern missions, served God faithfully for many years, while one of his sons seemed hopelessly confirmed in the life style of a reprobate. In a conference of ministers, 1,000 men of God felt moved upon to intercede for Carey's prodigal son. Very soon after that, Carey's prodigal returned. The time of his son's repentance was traced to the occasion of that great intercession that was lifted to the throne of grace for him. Jabez Carey not only returned to his father's faith, but later volunteered to labor in the most difficult mission field his father was working in and became a successful missionary in his own right.

It Will Work

Because our society as a whole has so devalued the idea of covenant relationships, parents may forget that the promises of God are immutable, which means "not capable of change." And the Scriptures teach, "It is impossible for God to lie" (see Heb. 6:18).

He has established His covenant with parents concerning their seed and their seed's seed. Abraham, Noah, and Job placed their confidence in the promise of God, not in the character of their children. They counted on God's character. That is a well-placed confidence that will bring what the Scriptures call the "rest of faith" (see Heb. 4:3).

As we have stated, the plan of God to bring our children into His purpose can only be realized through the exercise of faith. The Scriptures teach that without faith it is impossible to please God (see Heb. 11:6). We are not speaking of a "faith formula" of quoting Scriptures and maintaining a prescribed stance before God. The believing parent must cultivate the "rest" of faith that comes through quiet confidence based on God's assurance of what He will do for you, a parent in covenant with God.

Finally, no matter how it may appear to us at times, it is a part of God's plan that we wait for His promise. Waiting, in any realm, is one of the most difficult things for people to do. Waiting on God, in faith, is one of the ways that God uses to develop His character in us. God, in His great kindness, has even given us instructions concerning the temptation to become discouraged when the fulfillment of His covenant promises is not as we had anticipated:

> *For the revelation awaits an appointed time; it speaks of the end and will not prove false. Though it linger, wait for it; it will certainly come and will not delay.*
>
> Habakkuk 2:3 NIV

Notes

1. Charles Usher, *The Prayer Life*, (Fort Washington, Pennsylvania: Christian Literature Crusade, 1976), pp. 42-43.

Chapter 11

A Handful of Keys

We can be grateful that many who have gone before us have left a legacy of instruction relating to the nurture and training of children. Great men and women of God, among them William Booth, Andrew Murray, Susannah Wesley, and Count Zinzendorf, have had the foresight to leave for future generations their own philosophies and approaches that produced the fruit of sterling character in godly children. I have incorporated many of their concepts in my teaching over the past twenty years and have found that, when practiced sincerely, these principles still bear the same good fruit in children's lives.

I have also discovered that the spirit of the age in which we live is the greatest single detriment to rearing godly children. This fact has prompted me to reduce my philosophy for rearing godly children to a few powerful keys so that parents can easily grasp the most important principles. I want to make these keys available to parents, pastors, teachers, and leaders who desire to train and nurture children to find their own place in God's eternal purpose for them. As we distill the basic principles of concepts already discussed in this book, let's ask the Holy Spirit to let these keys of the Kingdom become realities to us to help us unlock the purpose of God for our children.

Key #1—Give your children a sense of destiny.

The first key the Moravians found, to produce children who would follow in their parents' footsteps and become missionaries to the ends of the earth, was to give them a *sense of destiny*. As you consider how you can give your children a *sense of destiny*, ask yourself, first of all, if this is number one on your agenda for your children. Put your name and your children's names in the place of generations of missionary families known to the Moravians: Beck, Hamilton, and LaTroke. Let your Becky, Ralph, or Sam be listed among those who gave their lives so that heathen nations could know the name of Jesus. Why should your children be ordinary? They were born to you, a Christian parent, and you have a call on your life to fulfill the purpose of God in the earth.

Are you convinced that there is nothing higher that your children could do than to be used of God in any way He chooses? That conviction will make them candidates for divine *destiny*. If you are convinced, then talk it! Live it! Expect it! Convince your children of the exciting possibilities that await them if they give their lives to God and live for His purpose. They will grow up with an exciting *sense of destiny*, knowing that they were born for a purpose and that God has specific goals for their lives.

Key #2—Preservation

Andrew Murray, in his book, *How to Raise Your Children for Christ*, writes:

> Too often Christian parents allow the world to prey upon their children. Oh, what thousands of children are thus drowned in the mighty Nile of this world! Would God that the eyes of His people might be opened to the danger which threatens His Church.[1]

After citing the power of the world as a negative force that threatens the lives of our children he makes this powerful and startling statement:

> It is not infidelity or superstition; it is the spirit of worldliness *in the homes of Christian people*,

> sacrificing their children to ambition or society, and to the riches or friendship of the world, that is the greatest danger of Christ's Church."[2]

If parents do not have a sense of destiny for themselves and for the lives of their children, it is inevitable that parents and children alike will be caught up in the spirit of the world. Its attractions will seduce them into thinking success is making a place for yourself "in the world" rather than in the Kingdom of God.

Moses' parents hid him in the bulrushes in an ark. The Bible says that they did this by faith. It is unbelief that refuses the responsibility to *preserve* children for God's purpose. Zinzendorf said that "from the cradle on, the souls should not know anything, but that they are created for Jesus, and that their whole joy be to know Him, to serve Him, to live with Him, and their greatest disaster would be, to somehow to be separated from him."[3] In a beautifully poetic way, he described that gift of life that God entrusted to your keeping when He gave you children: "They are precious hostages of grace, intrusted to the parents for the purpose of protection, nurture, and training." With such deep understanding of God's purpose for children, it is no wonder the Moravians *preserved* their children from worldly influences and experienced the joy of seeing them fulfill the purpose of God for their lives.

Key #3—The Key of Winning Their Hearts

Trying to rear godly children with strict demands of discipline is not the way to gain the desired results. We must begin by *winning our children's hearts*. Real love is not indulgence or hyper-attentiveness. And it does involve discipline. But without first winning the affections of our children, all our discipline will result in resentment against our unloving authority. We must win their affections to ourselves first if we are to win them to Christ.

Love, as it is experienced between parents and children, is a two-way street. It happens through eye contact and meaningful touch, as well as verbal affirmation. It is built through trust and sincerity and is perpetuated through forgiveness. It involves openness, letting them become a part of your life and showing them how much you appreciate who they are. And it must be genuine or children will know they are being patronized.

An "emotional home" is a relationship to which a person returns again and again with confidence and security. It is a place of unconditional love and acceptance established in agape love that is based on choice, not just feeling. The parents who build such a "safe" place for their children have *won their hearts*. Those children will trust their parents when they tell them of the claims of Christ and their need for salvation. In this way, parents will be able to win their children to Christ and His cause.

Five Key Words

In summary, let's hold five words in our minds that are powerful keys when applied to the development and implementation of our philosophy for winning our children to the Kingdom purpose.

Expectation

Expectation is a mentality that imposes itself in the direction of the person involved. Do you really have an expectation that your child will accomplish something special for God's glory? Of course, not all children will become missionaries or pastors. But do you expect that your child will live in the earth as salt and light—fulfilling the purpose of God to bring Him glory—no matter what vocation he or she chooses?

If we have a godly expectation for our children, they know they have something to achieve. Did your parents ever say to you, "I expect you to do this?" Didn't you enjoy their approval when you did what they expected? Or did you ever feel you had disappointed their expectations? Remembering those kinds of situations, we can relate to what a powerful key parental expectation can be.

Impartation

Part of equipping our children for Kingdom purpose involves the unselfish *impartation* of ourselves. This means in the simplest sense that we find a way to give them a part of the reality in God and in life that we have found ourselves. It can be a spiritual impartation of tender conscience or love for God and for others, as well as an impartation of natural wisdom or knowledge. It is passed from us to our children because we have a desire that they be equipped for the challenge that is before them.

This is why it is important to make your children a real part of your life. Whatever ministry area you are involved in, let your children be a part of that with you. For example, they can make visits to nursing homes, pray for the sick, or help you make Christmas baskets for the needy. It is important that your child be where the impartation is that you want him to receive. Careful! Impartation also works in the negative as well as the positive.

Education

Children must be properly *educated* in three realms of influence for them to be firmly established in godly principles: (1) in the home, (2) in the church and (3) in the school. If one of these arms of education contradicts the others, children will become confused, and they will be forced to choose between different value systems. Our church established a Christian academy because we don't want the world system in the public schools to undermine the Christian philosophy and training that we have invested in our children.

Children are to be educated continually in the home, as we saw in the biblical pattern in the Book of Deuteronomy, through every aspect of our lives (Deut. 6:6-7). Every life situation in our homes becomes an opportunity to teach about God and His ways. And we are responsible, as parents, to let our children become a vital part of the local church where God has "set" us as members of His Body (see 1 Cor. 12). In this way, they will learn to establish godly goals beyond their personal lives as they become effective members of the Body of Christ. The importance of identifying themselves as the Church, not simply attending church services, cannot be over-emphasized if children are to make serving God their priority in life.

Affirmation

Children need lots of positive strokes. *Affirmation* makes them feel that they are people of worth. They need affirmation from their parents, from Christian school teachers, and from members of the church. They need to be affirmed as a part of the vision God has given the church. If we provide a loving, accepting atmosphere for our children in these areas, giving them respect and proper attention, they are going to respond positively to the purpose of God.

We affirm the children in our church by making places for them to have expression. The children in our church pray, worship, sing, and are involved in most of the activities of our church. They are made to feel welcome and accepted by adults. We train them to be functioning parts of our church community life, not tolerated distractions. As we discussed in an earlier chapter, they are often involved in musical productions, dramas, nursing home visitation, and in helping with our conferences. They produce puppet shows, have Sidewalk Sunday Schools for the housing projects, and go into the local community with musical festivals involving dance and mime. They love overseas ministry, and on the teen level have done musical productions in Ukraine and Mexico. They feel a part because they are!

Consecration

This is a wonderful word because *consecration* doesn't just mean separated "from." It also means separated "unto." It doesn't mean that a child is simply isolated or insulated from the negative influences around him, but that he has been set apart for

God's will and purpose. He is in the world, but not of it. As parents continually yield up their children to be consecrated to the will and purpose of God, they are also providing the training that will make their children's consecration fruitful.

Through our children's and youth ministries in the church, we make a provision for our children where they are continually being led to fresh consecration. The children begin to understand that their vessels are for a higher purpose than their own desires, and that they must not allow themselves to be marred by the ungodly things of this life that do not promote that purpose.

Myles Monroe, who has written several books on purpose, made these three statements that will help keep you and your children on course:

(1) Without purpose life is a haphazard journey.

(2) Purpose gives existence meaning.

(3) Purpose gives precision to life.

Consecration to God's purpose for life will guarantee our becoming a part of God's eternal plan. And He has given us the keys to lovingly and prayerfully unlock that plan as we train our children in the way they should go. We understand that our children are God's creation. With the Bible as the instruction manual for His creation, with faith in our hearts, and with the Spirit of God teaching and guiding us, our children will become everything God meant for them to be.

Turning the Keys

When Jesus told Peter that He would give him the Kingdom keys, He specified keys *of* the Kingdom; not keys *to* the Kingdom (see Mt. 16:19). That meant that Peter had the keys that would enable him to *function* in the Kingdom according to the laws and principles God had established. To illustrate that principle, let's consider the personal set of keys I carry with me. They include my house key, my car key, my office key, and a master key to our ministry facilities. These keys enable me to function in those areas by letting me enter my house, drive my car, and have access to our facilities.

In that same way, keys of understanding biblical principles for rearing our children help us to function as parents according to God's principles. The *destiny key* opens the door to a future with promise. The *preservation key* will close the door to the wrong influences in our children's lives. And the *affection key* will keep them close to us so that our influence prevails over competing influences. How faithful the Holy Spirit is to give us all we need to help us and our children possess the land of promise.

Possessing the Land

There was much land to be possessed when Joshua took command of Israel. The previous generation left Egypt, a type of sin, and saw the promised land, but failed to enter and possess it. The present generation of young people is the Joshua Generation that God has marked to go into the land, along with everyone else who will take the challenge. Many parents have only eaten a few grapes that someone else brought them out of the promised land. This next generation will pay the price, receive the anointing, and enter the land themselves. They will rout the enemies, possess the land, and eat of the fruit of it.

Just as the angel came to the parents of Samson, so the prophetic word of the Lord comes to parents of children today who choose to be a part of this Joshua Generation. The angel instructed Samson's parents to rear him differently in order to equip him for God's purpose. If parents will take their responsibility prayerfully and seriously, the Joshua Generation will emerge before their very eyes, "strong and of good courage," free to manifest the power and purpose of God to the amazement of a sick and confused world. They will demonstrate the answers to a violent, promiscuous society that has begun to doubt their own ability to turn the world right side up.

The Joshua Generation—God's gift of light to a decadent age. It is our privilege as Christian leaders and parents to release them into His purpose, His power, and His plan.

Notes

1. Andrew Murry, *How To Raise Your Children For Christ*, (Minneapolis, Minnesota: Bethany House Publishers, 1975), p. 55.
2. Ibid.
3. Count Zinzendorf, *Articles on Children*, (Old Salem, North Carolina, Moravian library), translated from German manuscripts.
4. Ibid.

Kingdom Principles. A textbook for learning the basics of the Christian life, it contains the basic principles the author used to establish her ministry. It also continues to be a foundational text in the ongoing class for new members. Translated into many languages and distributed worldwide, *Kingdom Principles* is a simple yet comprehensive explanation of the Christian life.

To order send $7.00 plus $1.00 postage for each copy to:

SHEKINAH MINISTRIES
394 Glory Rd.
Blountville, TN 37617

The Forgiving Church. This book provides churches and individuals with practical help for answering Jesus' call to become a "forgiving church" by presenting issues that each of us must address. Pastor Curran probes deeply into our responsibilities as Spirit-led Christians as she explores the scriptural foundations for forgiveness in people's relations. She shares from her personal experiences and offers fresh insight into some of Jesus' most radical proclamations regarding forgiveness. The helpful and practical strategies this book offers will help our life styles better reflect our beliefs in this important area.

To order send $6.00 plus $1.00 postage for each copy to:

SHEKINAH MINISTRIES
394 Glory Rd.
Blountville, TN 37617